DESIGN FOR BUSINESS

Design for Business
edited by Ken Cato
Copyright c 1987
by Graphic-sha Publishing Co Ltd

ISBN 4-7661-0422-6

Manufactured in Singapore
First edition November 5 1987

Graphic-sha Publishing Co Ltd
1-9-12 Kudan-kita, Chiyoda-ku
Tokyo 102, Japan
Telephone (03) 263 4318
Telex J29877 GRAPHIC
Facsimile (03) 263 5297

DESIGN FOR BUSINESS

CATO

本書は、デザインが企業のイメージの向上にいかに大きく貢献しうるかを示している本である。イメージの向上を説明する言葉として、私はよく「イメージパワー」という表現を使うが、この言葉は企業内のあらゆる機能を結びつけて、市場にその存在を主張するような働きを言いあらわすときに用いられる。つまりこの本は、デザインがいかに商品の販売に影響を持ち、消費者の注意をひきつけ、見る者を触発し、力づけ、説得する力を持ちうるかを示しているのである。

「イメージパワー」は、コミュニケーションの場の獲得のために、日々熾烈な戦いが行なわれる中で、影響力と注意をひきつける力を持つ有効な手段である。

デザインスタジオのスタッフとしてのわれわれの役割は、単に視覚コミュニケーションを創造するという立場を、はるかに超えたものを要求される。われわれは、企業の理念と活動範囲を明快なかたちにし、その企業の存在をヴィジュアルにアピールする責任を負っているのである。

民間企業では、「企業に関する情報を伝える」という役割を持つものは、すべて何らかのデザイン処理を必要とする。その表現のかたちを美的にコントロールするのは、デザイナーの責任である。

デザインが人々の思考法に影響を与えているのは、もはや疑いようのない事実である。デザインは、マーケッティングの重要な手段であり、日毎に激しさを増していく商品競合の中で、大きく優位を占めるための手がかりである。人々は無数の日用品やそのパッケージとともに生活している。どこにいっても、視覚コミュニケーションの材料が目に入ってくる。このような情況下において、各商品が同一レンジの中で一貫したデザイン要素を持つというのは、至極当然のことになってくる。

本書に掲載された多数のデザインプロジェクトは、それぞれに意義があり、見る者に強い印象を与えた作品ばかりである。人々がその商品を買う際に、その決定に直接影響をおよぼした実績を持つデザインが、ここには紹介されている。

本書による説明をいくらしてみても、企業の利益となるものを明確に提示することはできない。正しいアイデンティティの開発という投資を行なってこそ、それは可能なのである。

その時にこそ、「イメージパワー」が完全に発揮されるのである。

INTRODUCTION

This is a book about the contribution design can make to the power of the image projected by a company and its products. Image power is a phrase I use to describe the dynamic presence a company can create in the marketplace by combining every aspect of its operation. Here, the role of design is to influence, arrest, inspire, encourage and persuade

Image power is a real and measurable corporate tool with the potential to influence and attract attention in a world where the space to communicate is contested fiercely

As a design studio, our role is far greater than simply creating visual forms of communication. We are vested with the responsibility of communicating a company's visual presence

In private enterprise societies, everything created to communicate information about a company is designed and it is the responsibility of designers to control this form of expression effectively in an aesthetic way

There is no doubt that design influences the way people think. It is a powerful marketing tool and can be used to great advantage in an increasingly competitive world. People are expected to live with a vast number of everyday household packaged products, their eyes are assailed by visually demanding communication pieces wherever they look and it is reasonable to demand that these items demonstrate integrity of design

The work pictured on the following pages is diverse yet every project is meaningful, memorable and has a real bearing on the way each company is perceived by its audience. Each design creates a powerful, individual impression which has directly, and measurably, influenced the purchasing decisions of consumers

No amount of explaining can communicate the benefits a company and its products can gain by investing in the development of the right identity

Only then will its image power be fully realised

Ken Cato

ケン・ケイトー・デザイン・カンパニーは、一九七〇年の創立以来、トータルアイデンティティプログラム、パッケージ、エディトリアル、プロモーション関係、建築グラフィック、サインなどを中心に仕事をしてきた。

現在われわれは、南半球最大規模を誇るデザイン会社に発展し、オーストラリア、シンガポール、香港、日本、韓国、中国、ニュージーランド、インド、パキスタン、パプア・ニューギニア、アメリカ、ヨーロッパを含めた一六ヶ国の企業や団体の、様々なデザインプロジェクトに取り組んでいる。

オフィスは、メルボルン、シドニー、シンガポール、香港、東京、アメリカにそれぞれ設置されている。

この国際性という要素において、われわれは明らかに他社に一歩先んじている。われわれはまた、視覚コミュニケーション戦略の手段として、日々増大する企業と市場の要請に見合った効果的なデザインを開発することにおいても、業界をリードする立場にある。

それぞれのプロジェクトの基盤となっているのは、最終段階において、安心感と完璧さをもたらすような、デザイン要素の選択と採用である。従ってどの作品も自信を持って完成させたものばかりである。またわれわれの企業理念は、新生面を拓く努力と、創設者ケン・ケイトーの経験から生まれた客観性に根ざしている。ケン・ケイトーは、AGI、AIGA、オーストラリアインダストリアルデザイン評議会、オーストラリアデザイン協会のメンバーであり、国際的なデザインの発展・普及のために、活発に活動している。

CATO DESIGN INC

Since its inception in 1970, Cato Design Inc has focused on the development of total identity programs, consumer goods packaging, editorial design, promotional literature, architectural graphics and signage

It is now one of the largest design companies in the Southern Hemisphere and is currently engaged in a variety of design projects for companies and organisations in 16 countries including Australia, Singapore, Hong Kong, Japan, Korea, China, New Zealand, India, Pakistan, Papua New Guinea, the United States and Europe

Cato Design Inc has offices in Melbourne, Sydney, Singapore, Hong Kong and Tokyo and in the United States

International in essence, the company has a strength which is evident in the look and feel of the work. As a strategic manager of visual communication, it is leading the field in the development of effective visual solutions to meet increasingly demanding corporate and marketing objectives

Underlying each project is a graphic discipline and control which is demonstrated in the final result with a sense of assuredness and completeness. Each article produced has its own aura of confidence. The philosophy of the company incorporates an eagerness to innovate with objectivity borne of the experience of its founder, Ken Cato. A member of Alliance Graphique Internationale, the American Institute of Graphic Art, the Australian Industrial Design Council and the Design Institute of Australia, Ken Cato is also active in furthering the development and dissemination of international design

THE BUSINESS OF DESIGN

In business, design decisions are made all the time, consciously or unconsciously. Office furniture, office equipment, paint colours, light fittings and floor coverings are all chosen as much for the way they look as the way they perform. The arrangement of all these elements within a space to best facilitate the function of a business requires a consideration of design. The clothes staff either choose or are paid to wear have been designed. A company's products and services have been planned and developed. They have been designed to achieve particular results. Design, in its broadest sense, contributes to every aspect of a company's day to day operation

To view design in an overall sense allows the development of a conscious design philosophy, accurately complementing and reflecting the company as a whole

A company's identity is fundamental to communication yet its corporate identity and its visual identity communicate on different levels. Corporate identity is inherent, arising from the philosophies of the people who run the company. It is not simply a subjective assessment of the way a company looks but is very much to do with inner qualities. A company can question what it is doing, it can define its goals and can structure the way it operates

Visual identity is a company's external persona and includes everything able to be controlled by designers. Not just graphic designers but architects, interior designers, industrial designers, fashion designers. Their tasks should not be a collection of independent interpretations communicating different messages. They are elements of the overall impression gained by the people to whom the company is presenting itself. If the elements have no visual cohesion, the company will not establish a unified identity. It is not unlike an orchestra where each musician contributes expertise in the playing of one instrument and the resulting sound is the achievement of a melodious harmony

Having a clear understanding of a company's personality is an important, integral factor in achieving the right visual identity. After all, the company's philosophy is the source of the ideas for the design program. Its actions, consistency and dependability are the factors that earn it recognition and success and these factors ought to be reflected with an aura of confidence

In what is essentially an organisational role, the designer develops the visual style of the communications material the company produces. Usually, it is a lengthy, complex venture handled jointly between management and design consultant and is therefore reliant on a spirit of cooperation between the two. The company provides accurate information on all aspects of its operation, including its philosophy. The designer contributes his experience in dealing with aesthetic problem solving and the direct communication of the solution. The success of the program depends on the level of contribution each party is prepared to make

As the needs of businesses have become more and more diverse, it is important for a design company to employ an individual approach and develop a unique and appropriate style. In other words, to use images in a meaningful and highly disciplioned way with the objective of directing a company's image power towards the most profitable end. Client needs, business categories, marketing strategies as well as consumer preferences and perceptions all demand to be considered individually

Without a coordinated visual design program, a corporation's stationery, publications, products, packaging, vehicles, premises and signage are very often diverse and bear little relation to one another. A company's first step in preparing for a visual identity program is to assess the fundamental strengths and weaknesses in the design of its products, packaging, stationery and other communication pieces. An effective visual identity can only be developed on a solid foundation of good design specifically prepared for individual items

Tangible proof of a strong, cohesive image also provides an important internal benefit because it gives shareholders, management and employees a greater sense of satisfaction and belonging

Design is not everything but a part of the overall corporate strategy and therefore, is a resource that should dramatically support a company and its products. Ultimately, our aim is to make design pay its way, by not only having a positive influence on the many esoteric aspects of a company's business but also influencing sales and profit

企業のニーズがますます多様化している現代において、デザイン会社は一つ一つのプロジェクトに対し、それぞれのアプローチを行ない、個性的かつ適切なスタイルを生み出すよう要求されるようになってきている。言いかえてみれば、企業の「イメージパワー」を最も有益かつ適切な方向へ向けるためには、きちんと系統立てて考えられた方法で、イメージを扱うことが大切なのである。クライアントのニーズ、ビジネスのカテゴリー、マーケット戦略、消費者の志向と感覚、すべて個別に検討していかなくてはならない。

一貫したヴィジュアルデザインプログラムがない場合、オフィスで使う事務用品、印刷物、商品、パッケージ、業務用車輌、建築、インテリア、看板等が、ばらばらのデザインで、一貫性を欠いていることがよくある。ヴィジュアルアイデンティティプログラムをとり入れるにあたって、企業が最初にすべきことは、商品やパッケージ、事務用品といった情報伝達のための道具のデザインに、どういう長所と短所があるかをつかむことなのである。効果的なヴィジュアルアイデンティティとは、一つ一つのものにそれに合ったデザインを施すという、強固な基盤の上に立ってはじめて、開発、達成される。

一貫したデザインシステムは、株主や経営陣、従業員に、満足感と帰属感を与えるからである。一貫した安定したイメージを持つことは、企業内においても、大きなメリットを持つ。

力強く安定したイメージを持つことは、企業とその製品を大きく支援する一つの動力だからである。そしてわれわれの究極の目的は、企業活動の多くの意義深い側面に積極的に関わるだけでなく、販売、および収益にも影響力を持つデザイン、つまり「ペイする」デザインを開発することなのである。

デザインとは、トータルな企業戦略の一部であり、デザインがすべてであると言いきることは、もちろんできない。デザインとは、

ビジネスの世界では、意識的にであれ無意識にであれ、デザインについていつも決定が下されている。オフィスの机、椅子、設備、室内の壁などの色、照明、床に何を敷くかなど、どのような効果をもたらすかを考え、すべてどのように映えるか、どのように合致する機能に最もよく合致するよう配置するためには、デザインをよく考えなくてはならない。職場内で着用する衣服についても、制服であれ私服であれ、デザインの考慮という段階を通過している。企業の製品やサービスも、設計、計画、開発にあたっては、特定の目標を達成するように「デザイン」されている。このようにデザインは、その最も広い意味において、企業の日常業務すべてに関っているのである。

デザインを広い視野でとらえると、その企業全体を正確に反映し、足りないところを補うような、鋭敏なデザイン哲学を持てるようになる。

企業のアイデンティティは、コミュニケーションの基本ではあるが、そのコーポレイトアイデンティティと、それを視覚化したヴィジュアルアイデンティティとは、異なるレベルで関連しあうものである。コーポレイトアイデンティティは、企業を運営する人々の信念が生み出す固有のもの、そして企業の外観について他社が持つ評価以上のもので、企業の内的資質と深く関っている。すなわち企業とは、その行動を自らに問いかけ、目標を設定し、運営の方式を決めるもので、これが先の内的資質にあたる。

しかし、ヴィジュアルアイデンティティは、企業が外部と接渉する際の仮面であり、デザイナーがコントロールしうるすべてを含む。この場合のデザイナーとは、グラフィックデザイナーだけでなく建築、インテリア、インダストリアル、ファッション、すべての分野の専門家が含まれる。だからといって、発注された仕事は、企業のアイデンティティについてのバラバラの解釈、異なるメッセージの寄せ集めであってはならない。各デザイナーが担当するのは、企業の姿を受けとめる人々が持つ、全体的な印象の各要素である。各要素間に視覚的凝集力がなかったら、統一されたアイデンティティを作り上げることはできない。それは、ひとりひとりの演奏家が、それぞれの才能を発揮して楽器を演奏し、美しいメロディとハーモニーを醸し出すオーケストラと似ている。

クライアントの性格をはっきり理解することは、適切なヴィジュアルアイデンティティを作り出す上で重要であり、欠かすことのできない要素である。理解をする上で必要なのは、企業の経営理念がアイディアの源になると認識することだ。ヴィジュアルアイデンティティは、その企業の活動、一貫性、信頼性は、会社が成功し、評価を得るための必要条件である。

こうした条件を確実に反映したものでなくてはならない。デザイナーは、オーガナイザーの一員として、クライアントである企業から提出されるコミュニケーションのための材料から、視覚的なスタイルを開発していく。それは、デザイナーと企業の経営陣が力を合わせて取り組む、長期にわたる複雑な作業である。従って、両者の協力の精神がきわめて大切な条件になってくる。企業側は、自らの経営理念を含め、活動のすべての面にわたって正確な情報を与え、デザイナーは与えられた課題に美的な解法を見い出し、それをダイレクトに表現するよう、自分の経験を提出するのである。つまり、プロジェクトの成功は、両者がどの程度まで情報交換できるかにかかっているのである。

PACKAGING

In its simplest form, packaging differentiates one product from another. People adopt a kind of individual packaging by wearing their choice of clothing to identify themselves as they wish to be seen. In much the same way, packaging design allows the designer freedom to develop an individual identity for a product and, at the same time, reinforce the product's attributes.
A package can then take the place of personal contact. It speaks for itself and an articulate package talks to all the senses: to taste, smell, hearing, sight and touch

It sells itself more eloquently than reams of advertising copy. In fact, it can provide the basis for more outgoing and imaginative advertising as long as it takes into account these four considerations: function, aesthetics, protective characteristics and cost of production. While the aesthetic aspects are important, it is more important to first meet the functional criteria. Aesthetic considerations are of necessity a matter of form following function, a notion in keeping with our 'right first, wonderful second' philosophy

A well designed package is a most effective marketing tool and a keen weapon in the struggle for market dominance. The struggle grows more fierce every day. No longer will a paper label create the difference required in a competitive marketing situation. Each element in the makeup of a product works in harmony as a total unit. A good package informs and improves upon one's knowledge of the product. It goes to the heart of the product and uncovers its reason for being in an eyecatching, easily understood way. At the same time, it will aim to satisfy the practical issues such as marketing objectives, legal requirements, the usage situation, the product's position in the marketplace, the way in which the product is displayed and its storage needs

A package is not merely an article wrapped up. A package is the sum total of the product's design, the materials from which it is manufactured, the design of its container and the application of graphics. A package is a complete piece of communication about the article it encloses. An article doesn't become a product until it is packaged. From the consumer's point of view, the package is the very basis on which the decision to purchase is made

Package shape is an important design consideration too often overlooked by designers. A package shape is a highly effective medium in which to create perceptual differences between products in the same category and to establish a product's identity. Tissues, washing powder and coffee are good examples of products that rely specifically on packaging for their identities. The shape of the package designed to contain these products not only distinguishes one from another, it may make the product easier to handle, easier to use or may be more cost-effective. The design of new package shapes has become a key factor in the immediate identification of particular products

パッケージとは、単に「包む材料」ではない。商品のデザインや原材料、容器のデザイン、グラフィックの使用といった様々な要素の総計であり、それが内に包むものについて情報を伝達する、それ自体で完成したものなのである。一つの製品は、パッケージデザインを施してはじめて商品となる。消費者からすれば、パッケージとは、買おうという決心をするそのもとにあるものなのだ。

パッケージのかたちは、デザインをする上で大切な要素なのに、デザイナーたちは実に簡単にその重要性を見のがしてしまう。この「かたち」は、同じカテゴリーの製品に感覚的な差異をつけ、きわめて効果的な媒体で商品としてのアイデンティティを築く、あるにもかかわらずだ。ティシュペーパー、洗剤、コーヒーなどは、パッケージにそのアイデンティティの主張を依存する商品の好例である。こうした製品を入れるためにデザインされたパッケージのかたちは、他の商品から自らを区別するだけでなく、扱いやすい、使いやすい、あるいはコストをおさえるなどの効果を持つ。パッケージのかたちを新しくデザインするということは、とりもなおさずその商品を他と区別し、すぐそれと見分けるための、中心的な役割を果たすということなのである。

パッケージは、どんなに簡素なものでも、それぞれの商品に合ったかたちで作られている。人間も、他の人からどう見られたいかを考えて、着るものを決めるというかたちで、自らの「パッケージ」を選んでいる。パッケージデザインの選択も、この人間の基準とよく似ている。

デザイナーはある商品のために、その属性を強調しつつ、独自のアイデンティティを開発する自由を持つ。デザイナーがそれに成功すると、パッケージは受け取る側とパーソナルな接触を始めるのである。適切精確なパッケージは、われわれの五感に——味覚に、聴覚に、視覚に、触覚に、直接語りかけてくる。

パッケージは、何百行のコピーよりも雄弁に、商品を売り込んでくれる。事実、機能、美しさ、商品の保護、および製作コストの四条件を十分に考えさえすれば、パッケージは想像力豊かな、親しみやすい宣伝材料となる。このような一触即発の状況下では、紙のラベルだけでは求められている差異を生み出すことはできない。一つの商品のそれぞれの要素は各々作用しあい、全体的なまとまりとしての調和を生み出す。すぐれたパッケージは、その商品について情報を与え、その商品の核心をとらえ、目につきやすく理解しやすい方法で、その存在理由を告げてくれるのである。

すぐれたデザインのパッケージは、マーケティング戦略上きわめて効果的な手段であり、市場において大きなシェアをかちとるための鋭利な武器である。シェアをめぐる競争は、日に日に熾烈さを増している。このような差異を生み出すことはできない。

満たしているということはもっと大切だ。二番目に挙げた美しさという条件も重要だが、機能を満たしているということはもっと大切だ。美しくという配慮は、必ず機能の次に来る問題で、われわれは「まず適切さ、それから素晴しさ」という哲学を持っている。

既存の情報に対しては、さらにくわしいデータをつけ加える。それはかりかその商品の核心をとらえ、目につきやすく理解しやすい方法で、その存在理由を告げてくれるのである。

と同時に、マーケティングの目標、法律による品質表示、使用法、市場における地位、取扱店内における展示や保管の方法などの実際的な要請をも満たす。

MACQUARIE
BANK

MACQUARIE BANK LIMITED

Macquarie Bank is a trading bank established following the restructuring of Australia's financial market. The bank is named after Governor Macquarie who introduced banking to Australia and the symbol is based on an innovative idea he had to increase the supply of currency in Australia's colonial days. He took silver coins, stamped out their centres and retained both pieces as currency. The larger coin became known as the 'holey dollar'. The corporate graphics and the interior of the bank have been carefully integrated. This is reflected in the consistent use of the corporate colours silver, black and grey and subtle patterns which appear in the decor as well as in documents such as cheques

マッコーリー銀行は、オーストラリアの金融市場再編成に伴い設立されたマーチャントバンク。植民地時代にオーストラリアへ銀行制度を導入した、マッコーリー総督にちなんで命名された。

シンボルマークは、通貨の流通量を増大するために総督が出した、革新的なアイディアにもとづく。それは一枚の銀貨の中央を大きくくりぬいて通貨を二枚つくることで、大きな方は「穴あきダラー」と呼ばれた。

コーポレイトグラフィックスとインテリアは、細心の配慮でコーディネイトし、企業色である銀、黒、灰色を使った繊細なパターンを、装飾や小切手などの用紙に一貫して用いてある。

Adele Palmer has a definite philosophy about her own fashions. Using highly textured fabrics, she layers them to create pattern on pattern with a splash of plain colour for a striking contrast. Her style allows fabric to change with the seasons but it is the way in which they are combined that creates her individuality. In designing a visual identity program for Adele Palmer, it was most important to communicate this aspect of her work. Using letters of varying weights from the same typeface, her name is positioned within a graphic 'statement' about her approach. It is used as the basis for a consistent yet changing identity for the range

アデル・パーマーは、自身のファッションについて明確な哲学を持っている。パターンの上にパターンを作り出すために、複雑な織りの素材を何枚も重ね、大胆な色をさっとあしらい、あざやかなコントラストを作り出す。彼女は季節によってファブリックに変化をつけているが、その組み合わせが非常にユニークで個性的である。ヴィジュアルアイデンティティプログラムでは、まず、アデル・パーマーの独自の手法をグラフィックで表現し、彼女の名前を同一書体の級数が異なる文字を使ってそこにはめこんだ。これをベースに少しずつエレメントを変化させて、ヴィジュアルアイデンティティブプログラムを展開した。

ADE**LE** **P**AL**M**E**R**

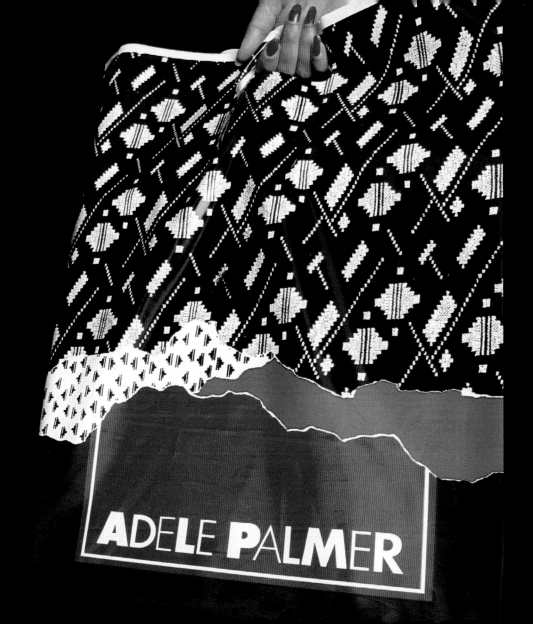

ADELE PALMER

SOUTH PACIFIC BREWERY LIMITED

South Pacific Brewery is the largest manufacturer of beer in Papua New Guinea. Three times in its recent history, the company has been awarded a gold medal in international competitions for the standard of its product. Now South Pacific beer is successfully exported to many countries around the world. Apart from quality, there are other major factors contributing to its success overseas. The mix of packaging, price and distribution are equally as important. The packaging design in this case became the visual identity with which the company was associated. The Bird of Paradise theme is striking and, with the addition of the palm trees and tropical island, is evocative of a drink from Paradise. At the same time, the design efficiently communicates the product's country of origin

サウス・パシフィック・ブルーワリーは、パプア・ニューギニア最大のビール醸造会社。ここしばらくの間に三度、国際的なビール品質コンテストでゴールドメダルを獲得している。世界の多くの国に輸出しているが、海外での成功の要因は品質はもちろん、パッケージ、価格、流通といった諸条件も重要である。パッケージデザインは、サウス・パシフィック・ブルーワリーのヴィジュアルアイデンティティになった。極楽鳥のテーマはそれだけでも目をひくが、ヤシの木と熱帯の島を組み合わせることによって、楽園の飲みものというイメージを更に喚起し、同時に生産国がどこであるかをも効果的に伝えている。

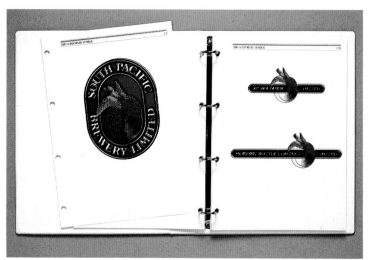

▮IDIOM

Idiom hand craft a range of high quality furniture which they market along with a number of imported pieces. We became involved in their future direction as they were designing their first showroom. It is a highly stylised, well designed space and is a true reflection of the capability and style of the company itself. Our task was to develop a name and an identity for what is now Idiom. The name reflects the company's individual nature as does the style of the logotype. The symbol reinforces their commitment to quality of design, a philosophy reflected in the furniture they produce. Both the logotype and the symbol have been used on signage, stationery, product folders and product information sheets

23

イディオムは手作りの高級家具メーカーで
輸入品も扱う。われわれはイディオムの
最初のデザインに参加し、将来の方向の
設定にかかわった。ショールームはよく
デザインされた高度な様式性を持つ空間であり、
イディオムの力量とスタイルを忠実に
反映している。われわれの任務は、社名を
考えアイデンティティを作ることで、
それが今のイディオムとなった。イディオムという名と
ロゴは、この会社の家具に対する
「デザインの質の追求」という信条を
力強く伝えている。ロゴとシンボルマークは、
看板、事務用品、製品カタログ、パンフレット
およびそれを入れるフォルダーにつけられている。

Grace Brothers is the largest chain of department stores in New South Wales and one of the largest in Australia. Recently, we were asked to develop a totally integrated and carefully planned revitalisation program for all of their stores. The company sells a vast range of goods from fashion items to white goods to fresh food and enjoys a very high and favourable awareness amongst all groups of consumers. Amongst its shoppers, there is a strong bias towards women. In developing a visual identity program for the company, it was important to take these considerations into account. The symbol we chose to represent the store is the New South Wales flower, the waratah, and although flowers are traditionally feminine, this symbol is also meaningful to a broad audience. The simplicity of the design is fresh and innovative and quite different from any other department store in Australia. The program involved the standardisation of the logotype and a consistent graphic presentation throughout all areas of the store's communication, from advertising to signage

グレイス・ブラザーズは、ニューサウスウェールズ州最大、オーストラリア屈指のデパートチェーンである。最近、全店舗をうまく統括できるように、綿密な活性化プログラムの開発をしてくれるようわれわれに依頼してきた。開発にあたっては、グレイス・ブラザーズがファッションからシーツ類、生鮮食料品に至る様々な商品を扱い、消費者の間で知名度も高く、良い評判を得ており、さらに顧客は女性が多いという事実を考慮した。シンボルマークには、ニューサウスウェールズの州花ワラターを選んだ。このため、更に広い層に伝統的に女性的なモチーフである花が、オーストラリアのデパートの中では訴える力を持つことになった。そのシンプルなデザインは、新鮮で革新的ですらあり、独自なものとなった。その他ロゴの標準化、宣伝から看板に至るグレイス・ブラザーズのグラフィック全領域を一体化した。

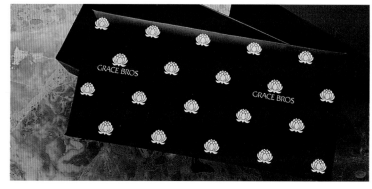

GRACE BROS PTY LTD

The visual identity program for Grace Brothers included the use of the symbol and logotype on store signage. For items such as hot and cold drink containers and supermarket shopping bags, we used the corporate colour in themes that were compatible with the program as a whole

ヴィジュアルアイデンティティプログラムの中には、シンボルマークとロゴを使って店内の標識をデザインする計画も含まれていた。あたたかい飲みものや冷たい飲みものを入れるコップやショッピングバッグのようなものには、プログラム全体に沿ったテーマをコーポレイトカラーで表現した。

DORF INDUSTRIES PTY LTD

Dorf manufactures and markets taps and associated products for both the plumbing trade and the public. The visual identity of the company has been established through the packaging. Most of the packages are printed in one colour on heavyweight cardboard to accommodate the weight of the products. The graphic treatment is simple and dramatic, and at the same time, informative. The products are represented in pictogram form and their dimensions are shown for easy identification. Dorf also makes a range of bathroom accessories. These design-oriented pieces gain added appeal through the use of photography

ドーフは蛇口の関連製品を作り、専門家と日曜大工の双方に供給している。

ドーフのヴィジュアルアイデンティティは、パッケージを通じて確立されている。

パッケージの多くは、製品の重量に耐える頑丈なダンボール箱に、一色で印刷されている。シンプルかつドラマチック、同時に十分に情報も提供するグラフィックである。中身はピクトグラムで示され、寸法もすぐにわかるようになっている。

ドーフは又浴室洗面所の関連製品も作っており、こうした製品はデザインが重要な位置を占めるため、写真を使って更に強くアピールするようにした。

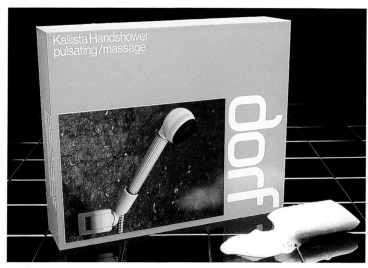

Pillar Tap

½" Booster, less handle and button

76

28

The Booster Pillar Tap combines
elegance and styling for basin and
trough applications in the laundry,
bathroom and ensuite.

Wall Swivel Outlet

7" Economy, Aerated

215

A wall-mounted swivel outlet for use in the kitchen and laundry

dorf

To develop a new visual identity program for a major airline is a mammoth task. In the relaunch of TAA as Australian Airlines, there were numerous major considerations to be taken into account. Perhaps the most important was the development of the new mark. TAA had used a kangaroo in their original livery and it was a symbol received very favourably by both staff and passengers, a fact strongly supported by research which showed there were sound reasons for reinstating it. In doing so, an abstract wing was incorporated above it to represent the company's function. The kangaroo and the word "Australian" are two of the most positive associations with the country. The colours were chosen to maintain continuity with the airline's heritage and to coincide with Australia's official colours of green and gold. The mark and logotype now adorn literally thousands of items produced by the airline to cover everything from airline offices to toothpicks

大きな航空会社の新しいヴィジュアルアイデンティティプログラムを作りあげるのは大仕事である。かつてのTAAをオーストラリアン航空として再提示しなくてはならなかったわけだが、その際最も重要視したのは新しいシンボルマークを作る過程であった。TAAの制服にはカンガルーのマークがつけられており、職員からも乗客からも大変評判がよかったし、調査の結果をみてもカンガルーはのこすべきだということになった。そのカンガルーの上に新たに、抽象化した翼をおいた。カンガルーと「オーストラリアン」という文字の組み合わせは、この国に最もふさわしい。色はTAAから受け継いだ緑と金。オーストラリアの国の色でもある。シンボルマークとロゴは、オフィスから実につま楊枝に至るまで、オーストラリアン航空の備品すべてにつけられている。

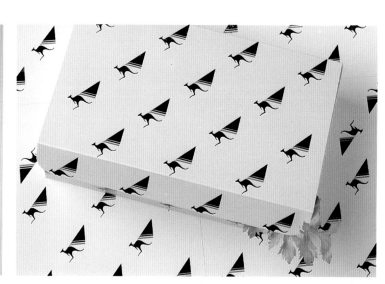

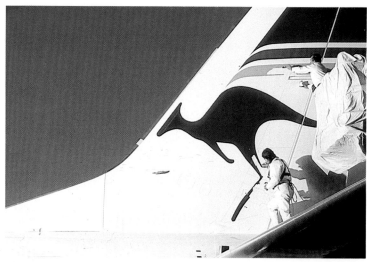

AUSTRALIAN AIRLINES (FLIGHT DECK)

Flight Deck is Australian Airlines' exclusive club for members and first class passengers.
The design program was developed around the symbol, an interpretation of the captain's
stripes. A simple and elegant mark, it is featured on airport signage, airport lounges,
membership cards, promotional folders and stationery

フライト・デックは、オーストラリア航空の会員およびファーストクラスの乗客のための高級クラブ。デザインプログラムは、キャプテンのそで章をあしらったシンボルマークを基本とした。シンプルでエレガントなこのシンボルマークは、空港内の看板やラウンジ、会員証、プロモーションのためのパンフレット入れにつけられている。

ASTRAL PACIFIC CORPORATION

Astral Pacific Corporation was formed as the result of a merger between two large New Zealand based companies, Progressive Enterprises and Rainbow Corporation Limited. To promote the bold, vibrant, confident personality of the new company, a visual identity program was developed around a simple, strong symbol depicting the company's position in the world. This was used on a wide range of material including stationery items and signage

アストラル・パシフィック・コーポレイションは、ニュージーランドに本社をおく二つの大手企業、プログレッシヴ・エンタープライズとレインボー・コーポレイション・リミテッドが、合併して生まれた新しい企業。その国際的地位を表現するため、簡潔で力強いシンボルマークをデザインし、それを中心に、この新企業の大胆さ、自信を反映したヴィジュアルアイデンティティプログラムを開発した。このシンボルマークは事務用品、看板などに使用されている。

ASTRAL PACIFIC

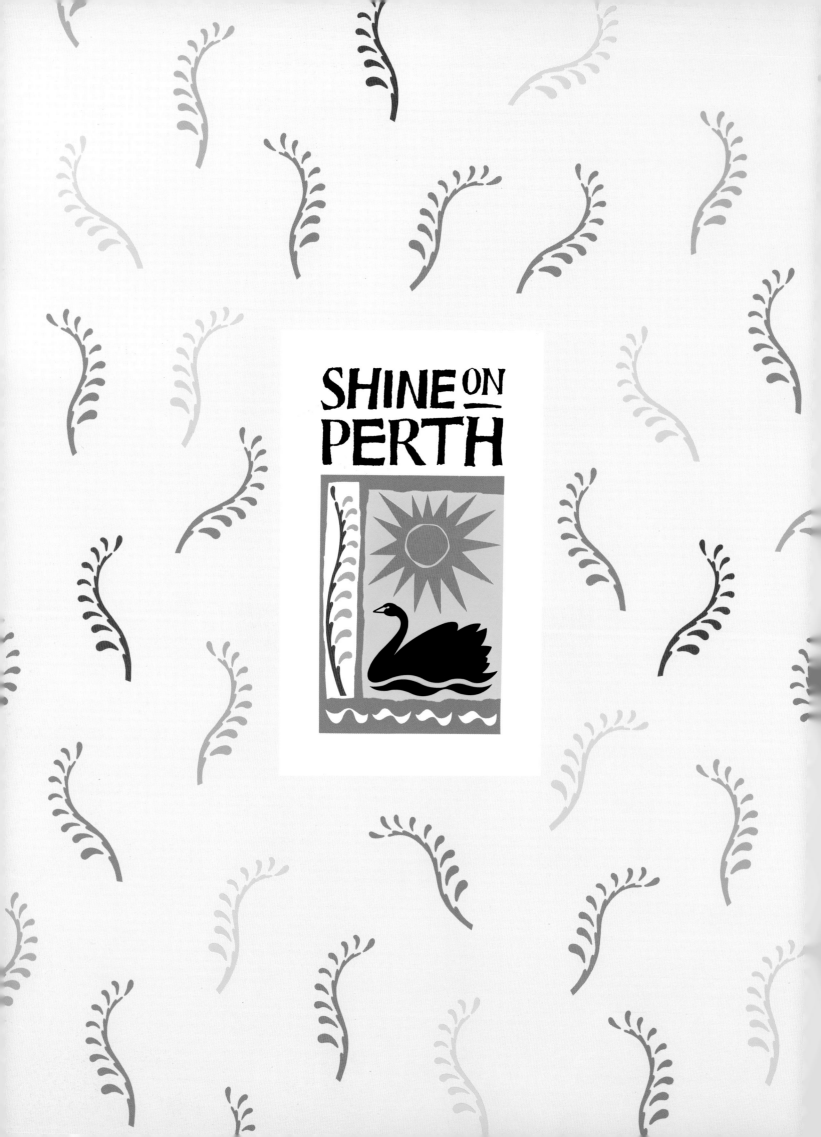

To promote the City of Perth, Australia, the city's council developed a theme, 'Shine on Perth'. Western Australia's symbol is the black swan, the state flower is the kangaroo paw and Perth's climate is usually warm and sunny. The visual identity captures all of these elements and has been designed for use on a vast range of material including press advertisements, stationery, pennants, t-shirts, posters, paper cups and souvenirs. The versatility of the design allows it to be used in one, two, three, four, five or six colours

西オーストラリアの州都パースはイメージの向上をはかるため、『輝くパース』というテーマをかかげた。西オーストラリア州のシンボルはブラックスワン、州花はカンガルー・ポー。そしてパースの気候は、あたたかく、日の光に恵まれている。ヴィジュアルアイデンティティプログラムはこの三つの点を採り込み、マスコミ向け広告、事務用品、ペナント、Tシャツ、紙コップや土産物に至るまで巾広い用途に耐えるデザインを行なった。デザインは色の面でも柔軟で、一色でも、それ以上六色までの色でも使用できる。

THE SWAN BREWING COMPANY LIMITED

The Swan Brewing Company is the major brewery in Western Australia. As the result of a major marketing decision to tackle the competition in the eastern states, the company undertook to upgrade their identity at every level, including redesigning their entire product range. Interestingly, their new visual identity has developed from the label design rather than the other way around. The symbol we developed uses the four colours from the original label. Black, red, gold and white have been used to create distinctly different products yet each works together to produce a powerful visual statement about the company

スワン・ブルーイング・カンパニーは、西オーストラリア州最大手のビール醸造会社。オーストラリア東部諸州市場の競争に参入する決断を下し、全製品のデザインのやりなおしなど、すべてのレベルにわたってアイデンティティをグレイド・アップした。面白いのは、新しいヴィジュアルアイデンティティはラベルデザインから生まれ、その逆ではなかったことである。われわれの作ったシンボルマークは、従来のラベルに使われていた四つの色を配している。黒、赤、金、そして白は他の製品とはっきり異なる存在を主張し、スワン・ブルーイング・カンパニーを視覚的に力強く訴えている。

Blue Cross manufacture a range of veterinary products suitable for a variety of animals. The symbol of the cross, pictured on the front of each package shown, evolved from the company's original packaging design. Pictograms of animals had also been used to communicate the purpose of the product range. Using these original ingredients, we developed a visual identity program that makes a very much stronger, easily identifiable statement about the function of the company. The interpretation of the blue cross allows immediate brand recognition which also is enhanced by the coding system created by pictograms of only the animals for which each particular product is intended

ブルークロスは、多種の動物用に巾広く獣医薬品を製造する。全製品のパッケージの表につけられた十字のシンボルは、もとのパッケージデザインからおこしたものである。前のデザインでは、製品の対象となる動物を明らかにするために使われていた。こうしたわれわれはもとからの素材を利用しながら、オリジナルよりはるかに強力で、簡単に見分けのつく主張しているヴィジュアルアイデンティティプログラムを作った。青い十字を見れば、すぐにどこのブランドかわかるようになっており、一つ一つの製品にその対象となる動物のピクトグラムをつけるコードシステムを採用したので、更にわかりやすくなっている。

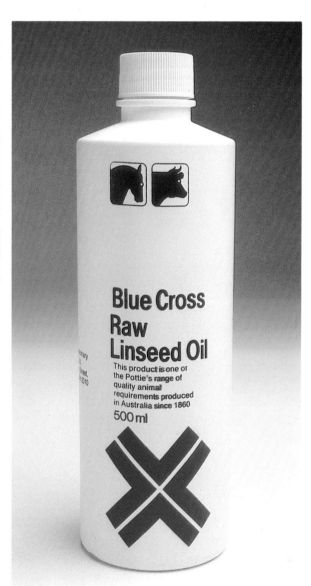

Blue Cross Raw Linseed Oil

This product is one of the Pottie's range of quality animal requirements produced in Australia since 1860

500 ml

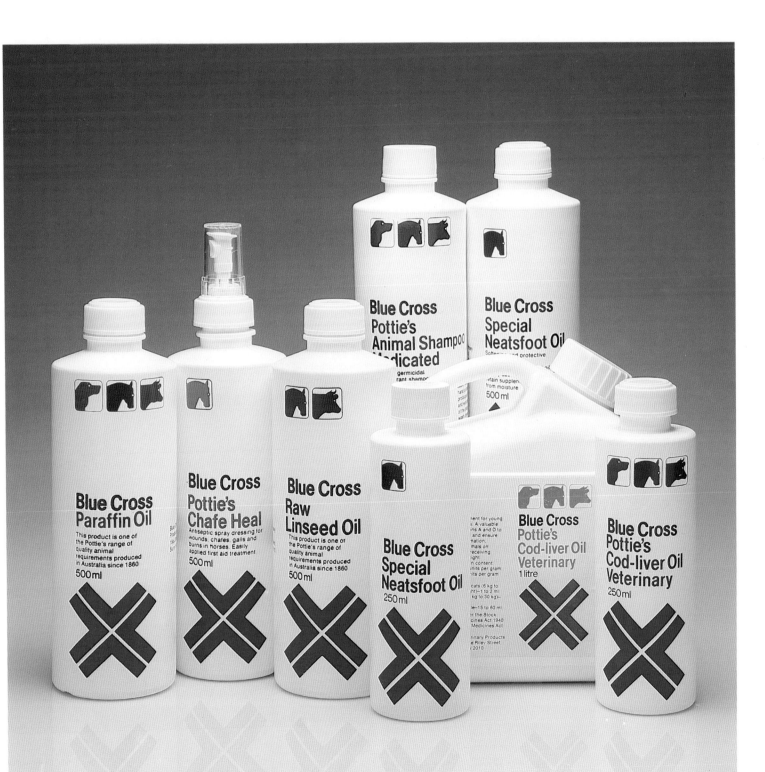

THE BEST TYPE *full*STOP

FULL STOP · 2nd FLOOR · 107 MOUNT STREET · NORTH SYDNEY · NEW SOUTH WALES 2060 · TELEPHONE (02) 957 6460 · FACSIMILE (02) 123 7891

PRINT PRO PTY LTD

Print Pro owns and operates a typesetting house under the trade name, Full Stop.
We developed an identity program for the company using a dynamic representation
of the name. The symbol appeared on a range of items, including posters, type books,
labels, business cards, stationery and T-shirts.

「フル・ストップ」は
プリント・プロの
写植会社。
アイデンティティ
プログラムは、
この社名を
大胆に表現して
いる。シンボル
マークは、ポスター、
書体見本帳、
ラベル、名刺、
事務用品それに
Tシャツに
つけられている。

VICTORIAN ARTS CENTRE TRUST

The Victorian Arts Centre complex is the premier venue for the performing arts in Victoria. The symbol design is based on the spire which is the predominant architectural feature of the centre, and is the linking element of the entire design program. It features on the outside of the building and all of the printed pieces relating to the centre. The design solution for the interior signage was to present the necessary typographic information on glass. This way, the information can easily be read and will not interfere with the many different wall surfaces. Individual identities were also created for the Melbourne Concert Hall, the State Theatre, the Playhouse, the Studio Theatre, the Performing Arts Museum, the Sidney Myer Music Bowl and the restaurants, coffee shop and bars within the centre

ヴィクトリアン・アーツ・センター・コンプレックスはヴィクトリア州第一級のパフォーミングアーツ会場である。シンボルマークは、センターの建築における特徴となる尖塔に基いており、デザインプログラム全体をつなげる役割を果たしている。このシンボルマークは、センターの建物の外側と、センター関係の印刷物につけられている。内部の標識は、ガラス板にタイポグラフィをのせて、必要な情報を伝えるようにした。こうすれば情報は簡単に読みとれるし、センター内の種々の壁面を邪魔することもない。メルボルン・コンサートホール、州立劇場、プレイハウス、スタジオシアター、パフォーマンスアーツ博物館、シドニー・マイヤー・ミュージックボウル、それにセンター内のレストラン、コーヒーショップ、バーにもそれぞれアイデンティティを作った。

GREEN
ROOM

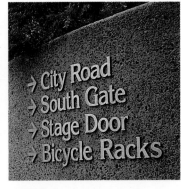

→ City Road
→ South Gate
→ Stage Door
→ Bicycle Racks

The Treble Clef

Victorian Arts Centre

→ Door 6

← Lift, Toilets
South Gate Exit
Door 5
Circle & Box A

4

Stage Door Level
Green Room
Staff Change Rooms
First Aid
ABC Control Room

THE VIC
RESTAURANT

VICTORIAN ARTS CENTRE TRUST

To create interest and to impart information about the events and activities offered by the Arts Centre, we produced the posters shown, for the Arts Centre itself, the Sidney Myer Music Bowl, the Performing Arts Museum and the Melbourne Concert Hall which is a subterranean venue, a fact reflected in the poster design

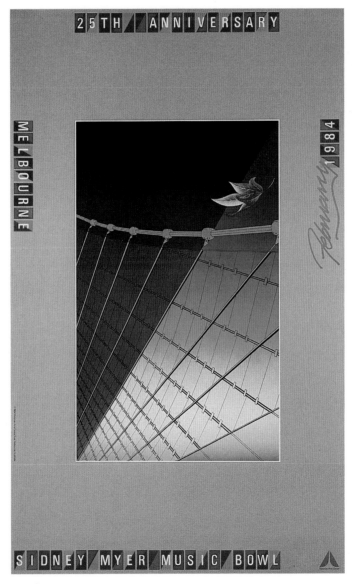

ここを訪れる人にセンターの
イベントや活動について
情報を伝え、関心を持って
もらえるよう、このページで
紹介しているアーツセンターや
シドニー・マイヤー・
ミュージック・ボウル、
パフォーミング・アーツ
博物館、それにメルボルン・
コンサートホールの
ポスターを作成した。
コンサートホールは地下に
あり、ポスターではその点も
表現してある。

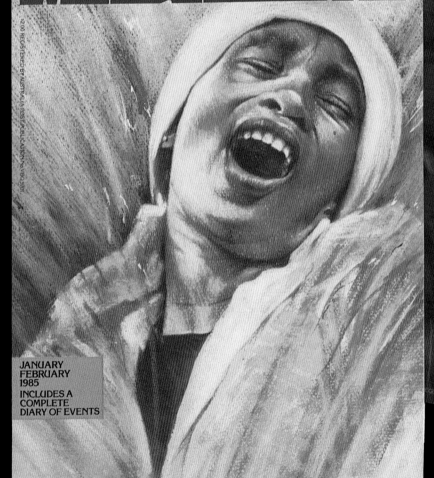

MAGAZINE
VICTORIAN ARTS CENTRE

REGISTERED BY AUSTRALIA POST PUBLICATION No VBG 5701

JANUARY
FEBRUARY
1985

INCLUDES A
COMPLETE
DIARY OF EVENTS

MAGAZINE
VICTORIAN ARTS CENTRE

AUGUST 1984
INCLUDES A
COMPLETE
DIARY OF EVENTS

REGISTERED BY AUSTRALIA POST PUBLICATION No VBG 5701

VICTORIAN ARTS CENTRE TRUST

The Victorian Arts Centre magazine is published monthly. Each issue contains a complete diary of events and reviews of the highlights. Our role allows us to control the design elements of the covers, each of which features a scheduled performer. Consequently, there is a strong and consistent theatrical theme unifying every issue.

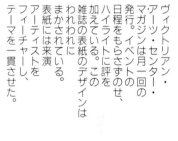

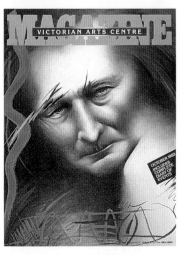

ヴィクトリアン・アーツ・センター・マガジンは月一回の発行。イベントの日程をもらさずのせ、ハイライトに評を加えている。この雑誌の表紙のデザインはわれわれにまかされている。表紙には来演アーティストをフィーチャーし、テーマを一貫させた。

ヴィクトリアン・アーツ・
センターは毎年一月、
メルボルンが静けさを
取り戻すこの時期に、
「メルボルン・サマー
ミュージック」という
イベントを開催する。
クラシック、ジャズ、
ポップス界の著名
アーティストや作曲家を
招待し、巾広い客層に
楽しんでもらおうというもの。
この写真の作品は過去
二回の同イベントに使われた。

VICTORIAN ARTS CENTRE TRUST

The Victorian Arts Centre runs an annual event called Melbourne Summer Music. It brings together eminent world renowned artists and composers from the classical, jazz and popular fields of music and its purpose is to attract a broad audience during January, a traditionally quiet period in Melbourne. Pictured is the material for two Melbourne Summer Music festivals

MELBOURNE SUMMER MUSIC

Nihon Siber Hegner manufacture a range of hearing products including ear plugs and ear muffs essentially for industrial situations. Our task was to develop a name and an identity for the range. The logotype uses letters of varying weights to show diminishing sound. The symbol reinforces this with a strong visual representation of diminishing sound waves. Shown here is the packaging we developed for the Earfit range, to be marketed in Japan exclusively

50

ニホン・サイバー・ヘグナーは、労働の現場で耳を保護するために必要な耳栓や耳おおいなど、一連の製品を供給している。われわれへの依頼は、この製品のシリーズに名前をつけ、アイデンティティを開発することだった。ロゴはさまざまな太さの文字を使って音が消えてゆくさまを示し、シンボルマークは消えゆく音波を強力に視覚化した。これは日本市場向けのイアフィットシリーズとして作ったパッケージデザイン。

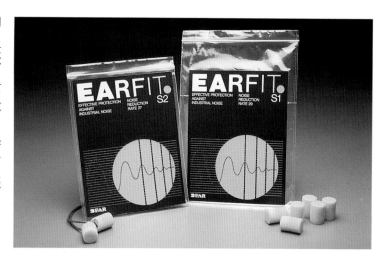

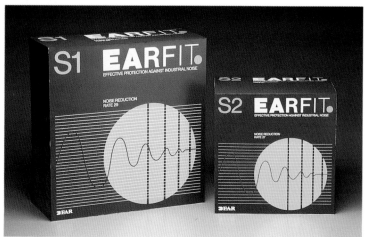

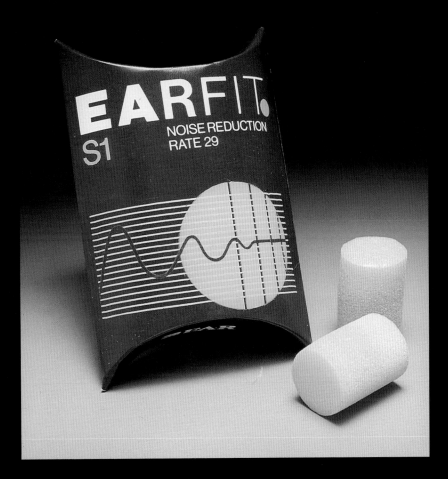

In the highly competitive coffee market, Andronicus is a proven brand marketed by Nestle. To develop a rejuvenated identity for the range, it was important to achieve a simple elegance to make Andronicus stand out from the rest and attract attention at point of sale. At the same time, the family look across the range is evident, yet each variety of coffee is clearly and easily identified

競争の激しいコーヒー市場で、ネッスルの「アンドロニカス」は競争力のあるブランドである。我々はこのシリーズでのアイデンティティの活性化を依頼されたが、「アンドロニカス」が他社の製品より目立ち、注意を引きつけるようにするためには、「シンプルなエレガントさ」が必要だった。また同時に、このシリーズの家庭的な外観を維持しながらも、それぞれのバラエティは明瞭に見分けがつくようにした。

SUSSAN CORPORATION (AUSTRALIA) LIMITED

The Sussan Corporation is a network of stores specialising in clothes designed for young women. We were asked to develop a program to revitalise the company's visual identity. The existing logotype was retained and integrated with a new symbol that is a vital image communicating style, colour and fun. Its bright highlights allowed the lettering in the logotype to be used more dynamically. The symbol has been used on carry bags, swing tickets, window signage and in catalogues. Literally, it has created a 'face' for the company

スサン・コーポレイションは若い女性向けのファッションを専門とするチェーン店。われわれは、そのヴィジュアルアイデンティティを活性化するプロジェクトを作るよう依頼された。そこでロゴはそのままのこし、スタイル、色、楽しさを伝えるようないきいきとしたシンボルマークにした。こうしてロゴのレタリングは、よりダイナミックに生まれ変わった。シンボルマークはキャリーバッグ、品質表示票、ショーウィンドウの看板、カタログに使われている。シンボルマークは文字通り、スサン・コーポレイションの顔となったのである。

BANK OF SINGAPORE (AUSTRALIA) LTD

The Bank of Singapore opened in Australia following deregulation. To gain awareness
in a new and highly competitive environment, it was important to develop a visual identity
program with powerful imagery. The symbol was adapted from the Singapore flag.
The crescent moon represents the emerging nation or in this case, the emerging bank.
Traditional Chinese colours of red (good luck) and gold (prosperity) lend the mark a
sense of depth and richness. The Bank of Singapore now has a strong yet simple identity
demonstrated on the broad range of banking forms, stationery items, public relations
folders and indoor and outdoor signage

シンガポール銀行は、オーストラリアの外国銀行に対する規制が緩和された後、オーストラリアで業務を始めた。新しい、競争の激しい環境で、知名度を高めるために、強力なイメージを持つヴィジュアルアイデンティティプログラムを開発する必要があった。シンボルマークはシンガポールの国旗からとり、新生国家をあらわす三日月はここでは新生銀行の含みをもたせた。中国の伝統色である赤（幸運）と金（富）を使い、深みと豊かさがそなわった。シンガポール銀行はこうして力強いアイデンティティを持つことになり、銀行業務用紙、事務用品、PR用パンフレット、事務用品、PR用パンフレットを入れるホルダー、室内室外の看板などに巾広く使われている。

BANK OF SINGAPORE

OF SINGAPORE

BANK OF
SINGAPORE

Cheque Book

The Advance Australia Foundation is a government sponsored initiative designed not only to promote Australian products to Australian people but to create an identity in export markets too. The promotion was launched in the second half of 1986 to help counter the effects of the decrease in the value of the Australian dollar. It was important to develop a symbol which could be instantly recognised as being Australian. The kangaroo is an obvious choice and here, it has been reproduced with refreshing simplicity. The triangle is reminiscent of 'A' for Australia and the whole has been designed in the country's official colours of green and gold

58

アドヴァンス・オーストラリア財団は、オーストラリアの生産物を国内で販売促進し、輸出市場においても商品地位を確立するべくオーストラリア政府の助成を得て設立された。一九八六年後半、オーストラリアドル下落の影響を最少限におさえようとして、この促進キャンペーンが始まった。このため、一目でオーストラリアのものとわかるシンボルマークを作る必要があり、当然のようにカンガルーがテーマとして選ばれた。こうしておなじみのカンガルーは、シンプルなデザインでよみがえることになった。三角形はオーストラリアの「A」を想起させシンボルマーク全体は、オーストラリアの色、緑と金でデザインしてある。

AUSTRALIAN EXPORT

AUSTRALIAN MADE

AUSTOTEL MANAGEMENT PTY LTD

Austotel is a consortium of three shareholders who own 296 hotels. Traditionally, Australian hotels have long been seen as the man's drinking domain. Austotel plan to eventually renovate 200 hotels to accommodate a broader market. Large windows and light colours will create a feeling of space and light, an atmosphere more appealing to women and a deliberate move away from the dark, den like atmosphere of the 'watering holes' of the 1950s. The symbol reflects this move. As an abstract 'A' it embodies the notion of a chain with connecting links. Represented in gold on printed material and brass on the front of each hotel, the symbol reflects a level of prestige and quality that is synonymous with the aims of the company

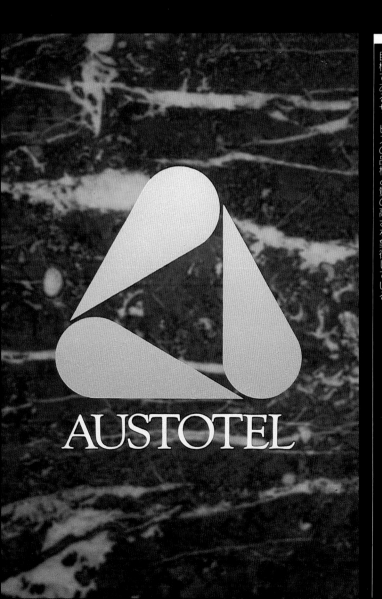

オーストテルは、二九六のホテルを持つ三人の株主が経営する合弁企業である。オーストラリアのホテルは、男たちが酒を飲みに集まる場所としての伝統的なイメージを持っている。オーストテルは市場を広げるため、最終的には二〇〇軒のホテルを改築する計画である。一九五〇年代の、暗くガブ飲みする場所、タバコの煙でいっぱいの小さな穴ぐらという感じを払拭し、大きな窓と明るい色で広々とした空間、明るい光を作り出し、女性にもアピールする雰囲気を作ることになっている。このシンボルマークもこの方針をあらわす。抽象化した「A」は鎖のつながりを反映する。それぞれのホテルの正面に金で刷り込み、印刷物に金で刷られたシンボルマークは、オーストテルの目標であるサービスの品格と質の高さを象徴している。

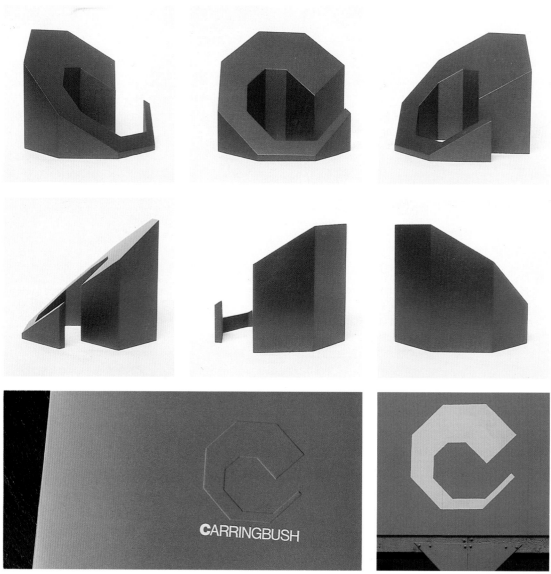

CARRINGBUSH PTY LTD

Carringbush is a property development company that has been responsible for an impressive number of architecturally interesting buildings on prime Australian city sites. To reflect their commitment to growth and the construction of quality developments, we designed a symbol formed by the letter 'C' that grows in a clockwise direction in segmented lengths to represent growth in stages. The symbol has been used on stationery and, in its varied form shown here, on building hoardings

カリングブッシュは、オーストラリアの都市の一等地に、建築学的に興味深い多数のビルを建ててきた不動産開発企業。カリングブッシュの追究する成長、および質の高い開発という要素を反映させるため、われわれは頭文字の「C」を基本にしたシンボルマークをデザインした。「C」は時計回りに分節されつつ伸びていき、段階的な成長を表現している。このシンボルマークは、事務用品や建設現場の板囲いなど様々なかたちで使われている。

AUSTRALIAN MUSIC CENTRE LIMITED

The role of the Australian Music Centre is to promote Australian music writers, locally and overseas. To this end, the Centre's library and information service contain a vast amount of music-related material. Our task was to design a visual identity program reflecting the Centre's commitment to its task. The bright, colourful symbol we designed is featured on stationery items, brochure and signage

オーストラリアン・ミュージック・センターの役割は、国の内外で活動するオーストラリアの作曲家をプロモートすることであり、センターの図書館および情報サービスには、莫大な量の音楽関係資料がある。われわれはその熱心な仕事ぶりを反映するようヴィジュアル・アイデンティティプログラムを開発した。明るい色どり豊かなシンボルマークは、事務用品、パンフレット、サイニッジに使われている。

Australian Music Centre

Until recently, Vegetable Oils Pty Ltd manufactured a range of cooking oils and margarines, including Meadow Lea, the largest selling brand of margarine in Australia. The product's high profile motivated the company to adopt its name for the entire corporation. Our task was to interpret the name's new role and develop a visual identity to reflect the corporate personality. The logotype is a warm, friendly, soft and round version of the product name and is compatible with the personality of the company.

We were also asked to look at the product itself. The top of the plastic tub containers is very strongly branded and, with improved printing techniques, it was possible to use the container sides to depict changing scenes, usually relating to Australia's history. These themes are compatible with posters produced by the company for schools

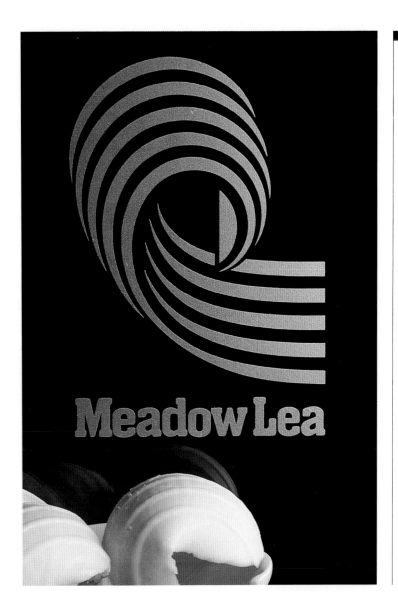

ベジタブル・オイル社は食用油メーカーである。その中でも「メドウ・リー」というマーガリンはオーストラリア最大のシェアを持つ製品だが、これがきわめてよいイメージを持っているために最近製品名を社名にするに至った。われわれは新社名の役割を考え、会社の性格を反映するヴィジュアルアイデンティティプログラムを開発するよう依頼を受けた。ロゴは、会社の性格に沿うものにした。同時に商品そのものについても親しみやすくあたたかく、まるみをもたせ、プラスティック容器のフタにブランド名を貼り、デザインを依頼されたので、プラスティック容器の側面にもオーストラリアの歴史上の名場面をよって、側面にもオーストラリアの歴史上の特殊な印刷技術にフタにブランド名をバンと貼りデザインを依頼されたので、よって、側面にもオーストラリアのフタにブランド名をバンと貼りデザインを依頼されたのでようにつけた。このテーマはメドウ・リーが学校絵巻物のように配るポスターと同じである。

AUSTRALIAN BICENTENNIAL AUTHORITY

To celebrate Australia's Bicentenary, a range of promotional material was developed based on the existing Bicentennial symbol. The theme of stripes was carried through to posters, banners, swing tags, pennants and point of sale items which were distributed throughout every state in Australia. The stripes were used as the basis of a visual identity program developed to reflect various people and events in Australia's history over the past two hundred years. In different weights, lengths and colours, the stripes helped to impart this historic occasion with a sense of vitality, excitement and interest. A specially designed 'striped' typeface was used on promotional material as a common element not only to communicate the Bicentenary but also to suggest the central symbol

オーストラリア建国二〇〇周年を祝うため、われわれは既存のシンボルマークを基本にさまざまなプロモーションマテリアルを開発した。シンボルマークの線のテーマは、ポスター、旗、建国二〇〇周年にちなんだ商品の品質表示札、セールスアイテムに使われ、オーストラリア全国に行きわたっている。線は、過去二〇〇年のオーストラリア史に登場する人物や事件をデザイン化して開発したヴィジュアルアイデンティティプログラムの基本になるテーマである。線のテーマは、太さ、長さ、それに色を変え、建国二〇〇周年のバイタリティ、エクサイトメント、インタレストといった雰囲気を表現している。特別にデザインした「線」のタイプフェイスは建国二〇〇周年を表現するだけでなく、シンボルマークともつながるもので、プロモーションマテリアルのすべてに使われている。

Australia
1788-1988

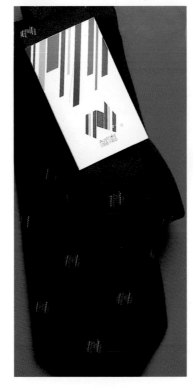

ROBERT TIMMS PTY LTD

Robert Timms is a leading marketer of coffee blends in foil packs, tins and sachets. The visual identity of the company has been through three major periods of transition, each one further developing the original creative strategy. The New Guinea Gold pack featuring the Bird of Paradise is the company's 'flagship' and its design has inspired a range of packs with bold, brightly coloured, exotic images against a black and gold background, the colours with which the company has become identified

ロバート・ティムズは、アルミパックカン入りと袋入りのブレンドコーヒーの大手メーカー。同社のヴィジュアルアイデンティティは、三回の大巾な変更を経験している。いずれも当初の独創的な戦略を先へ押しすすめたものである。極楽鳥を中心にすえた「ニューギニアゴールドパック」はロバート・ティムズの「旗艦」であり、黒を背景に大胆な明るい色のエキゾチックなイメージを配するという、一連のパッケージデザインの源泉となった。このパックの配色で、ロバート・ティムズはその名を知られるようになったのである。

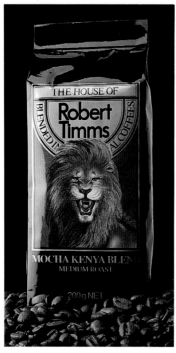

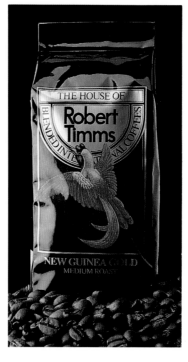

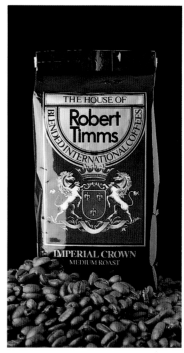

PURE COFFEE BEANS

NEW GUINEA GOLD

Robert Timms

BLENDED INTERNATIONAL COFFEES

200g NET

in this pack have been chosen from selected
a Gold formula by the House of R

LEVER & KITCHEN PTY LTD

Softly is a traditional wool wash, one of many household products marketed by Lever & Kitchen. The original pack concept was similar in look and feel to the pack pictured here. It simply needed updating. We retained the image of the caring mother with her child yet we presented them from a contemporary perspective. So while the image was still valid, it needed to be re interpreted for the product to retain a viable and, at the same time, familiar position

「ソフトリー」は伝統的な
ウール用洗剤で、リーヴァ・アンド・
キッチンが市場に出している
多くの家庭用品の一つ。昔の
パッケージコンセプトは、今回の
パッケージと外観も感じも変わらない。
ただ、時代に合わせる必要はあったので、
やさしい母親と子供というイメージは
のこしてそれを今日的な
パースペクティヴから表現した。
商品の昔ながらの地位を保ちつつ、
なおかつ親しみやすいものにするため、
そのイメージをもう一度見直す
必要があったのである。

NICHOLAS KIWI LTD

Nicholas Kiwi market a diverse range of household products including Prize, a liquid wool wash. This was an opportunity to create a very different look for the product. We were involved in the development of the pack shape and on the shelf in the supermarket, the message it conveys is clear and immediate. The simple label reinforces the product attributes

ニコラス・キイウイは、ウール用液体洗剤「プライズ」など各種家庭用品を市場に出している。われわれは、この「プライズ」のイメージを一新することをめざした。まずパッケージのかたちを変え、スーパーマーケットの棚の上でこの商品の存在がすみやかにはっきりと伝わるようにした。シンプルなラベルは、「プライズ」の特質を強調している。

The Australian biscuit market is highly competitive and Nabisco is one of its leading brands. Our task was to evaluate their vast biscuit range (including cookies, creams, chocolates, crackers and savoury biscuits) and develop a design program to give the company a cohesive and highly visible presence at point-of-sale. Each individual product required an identity. It had to be capable of standing alone yet still be seen to be part of the Nabisco 'family'. To achieve this end, it was necessary to take three major considerations into account. Firstly, the number and variety of products in the range; secondly, the powerful image developed by its major competitor and, finally, the limitations created by their existing logo design. In fact, the logo design became the catalyst for the visual identity program we created. The format we devised uses a highly disciplined approach to create a visual difference on the supermarket shelf. Our design, based on a diagonal line, allows every pack in the entire Nabisco range to be quickly and easily identified.

競争の激しいオーストラリアのビスケット市場にあって、ナビスコはリーディングブランドの一つである。われわれは、クッキー、クリーム、チョコレート、クラッカー、味つきクラッカーという各種広範囲にわたる同社のビスケット製品を吟味し、売り場でナビスコの存在を主張するようなデザインプログラムを作ろうとした。一つ一つの製品はそれぞれのアイデンティティを要求する。一つだけでも存在しうると同時に、巨大なナビスコ製品の一部であることもはっきり伝えていなくてはならない。そのために三つの点を考慮した。まず、全製品の数と種類。そして主な競争相手が作りあげた強力なイメージ。おしまいにそれまでのロゴの持つ限界である。実際はこのロゴデザインがヴィジュアルアイデンティティプログラムの触媒役を果たした。われわれは、スーパーマーケットの商品棚で視覚的な差異を生み出すようなフォーマットを厳選した。斜めの線を基本にしたデザインでシリーズの一つ一つのパッケージが簡単にすぐ見分けられるはずである。

The power of Nabisco's new consistent identity is flexible enough to be applied to all of their products, yet it allows for distinct product differences

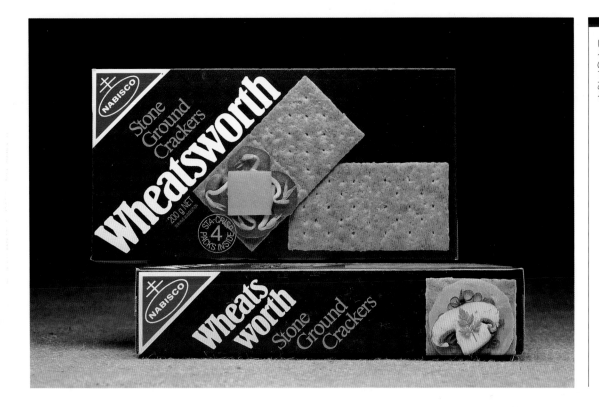

ナビスコの
新しい
トータル
アイデンティティの
力は、全製品に
適用が
可能である。
しかも
一つ一つの
製品の差異を
明確に
するだけの
柔軟性を備えても
いるの
である。

In Southeast Asia, it is customary to send Chinese New Year cards, particularly to business associates. Gibson Public Relations saw this as an opportunity to create and maintain a powerful presence. For several years, we have designed a series of large posters, each featuring a graphic interpretation of the coming Chinese Year. Pictured here are posters representing the Year of the Ox, Year of the Tiger, and the Year of the Rabbit

74

東南アジアでは、中国暦による年賀状を特にビジネス関係へ送る習慣がある。ギブソン・パブリック・リレイションズでは、これを自社のセルフ・プロモーションのよい機会と考えているので、われわれはこの数年間、中国暦の新年をグラフィックにした大型ポスターをデザインしている。ここで取り上げたのは丑年、寅年、卯年のポスター。

GIBSON

GIBSON PUBLIC RELATIONS (PTE) LTD
100 BEACH ROAD #25-01 SHAW TOWERS SINGAPORE 0718
TELEPHONE: 291 1199 TELEX: RS 38598 GIBSON TELEFAX: (65) 291 0460

THE TIGER, THE KING OF ANIMALS
IN THE EAST, POSSESSES A DIVINE ARMOUR,
AS MARVELLOUSLY STRIPED HOME ABOVE ALL, HE IS A SYMBOL OF LUCK,
POWER AND DIGNITY.

IN 1998, THE YEAR OF THE TIGER,
HIS STRENGTH MUST BE RESPECTED,

INSTINCTIVELY LOYAL AND
HONOURABLE, THE TIGERS' VIRTUES COMBINE
INNER STRENGTH, GRACE AND SELF CONTROL,
VITAL ATTRIBUTES FOR LEADERSHIP AND SURVIVAL IN THE
KINGDOM OF THE JUNGLE.

breaking the
sound barriers

**Consolidated
Electronic
Industries**

**Stereo
Cartridge
Systems**

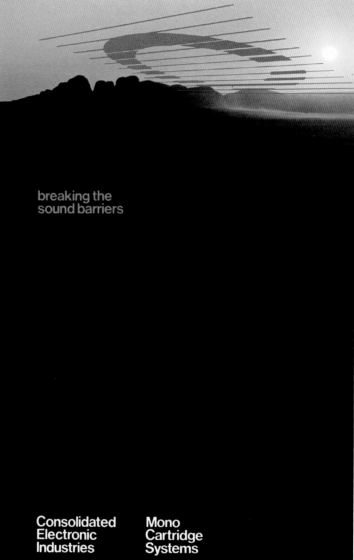

breaking the
sound barriers

**Consolidated
Electronic
Industries**

**Mono
Cartridge
Systems**

CONSOLIDATED ELECTRONIC INDUSTRIES PTY LTD

Consolidated Electronic Industries is a major supplier of audio and video equipment to production houses and broadcasting stations. In America, they built the first 24 hour self operating radio station. The company is innovative, technologically creative and undaunted by problems and limitations. We devised their corporate symbol to reflect their positioning statement, "breaking the sound barriers," and we have been able to use it flexibly to give dimension to this claim. Pictured are the covers from a series of brochures presenting the range of products designed and manufactured by CEI and related technical information. They formed part of a total corporate image program we prepared. The symbol, as shown below, was the basis for all the variations we developed

CEIは、オーディオ・ビデオ機材をプロダクションや放送局に供給する大手企業で、アメリカでは世界に先駆けて、二四時間完全自動放送ラジオ局を作っている。CEIは技術革新に敏感で、創造的であり、困難や限界をものともしない。われわれはCEIのモットー、「音の壁を突き破る」を反映するシンボルマークを作り、それを柔軟に使って、モットーに広がりを持たせた。これはCEIが設計・製造したオーディオ・ビデオ機材を紹介し、関連技術情報を盛り込んだパンフレットシリーズの表紙であり、われわれが作ったトータルCIプログラムの一部である。下のシンボルマークを基本にしてさまざまな展開を行った。

JURONG BIRD PARK (PTE) LTD

The Jurong Bird Park is one of Singapore's major tourist attractions and home to 3500 birds. It also features the world's largest walk through aviary. With so many birds, it was important to be non specific when developing an identity program for the park. The purpose of the symbol is to express an easily identifiable common element, a bird's wing. Its bright colours add a sense of fun and interest to the movement inherent in the image. Interpretations of the symbol have been used on a broad range of items, including the train to transport visitors around the park, attendants' uniforms, mailing tubes, stationery, calendars and flags. Banners for the front entrance to the park were also designed featuring particular characteristics of various bird species

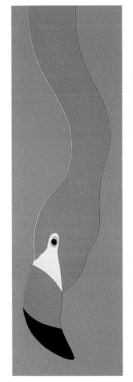

ジュロン鳥類公園は、シンガポールの大きな観光地。三五〇〇羽の鳥がいる。鳥舎は中を歩いて通れるようになっており、この種のものでは世界最大の規模を誇る。多種多数の鳥がいるため、アイデンティティプログラムを作る際には、かたよったイメージをさける必要があった。つまりシンボルマークはなじみのあるものシンボルマークをすぐわかるようにデザインした。明るい色を使ったので、鳥の翼から連想する躍動感に、楽しさと面白さが加わった。シンボルマークは公園で乗客を運ぶ列車や職員のユニフォーム、郵便物を入れる円筒容器、事務用品、カレンダー、旗などにあらわれている。入口正面ののぼりは多種の鳥の特性を盛り込んでデザインした。

Sunshine Allied Chocolate, based in Singapore, manufactures and retails fine quality chocolates under the brand name Le Chocolatier. The company also conducts franchised outlets in department stores and international airports. Our visual identity program included the development of the logotype, symbol and colour scheme, all of which were interpreted for store signage, packaging and stationery

シンガポールに本拠をおくサンシャイン・アライド・チョコレートは「ル・ショコラティエ」のブランドで高級チョコレートを製造販売し、デパートやいくつかの国際空港にも販路を持つ。われわれはロゴ、シンボルマーク、色彩設計などのヴィジュアルアイデンティティプログラムを作成した。ロゴ、シンボルマークは店の看板、パッケージ、事務用品に使用された。

MIMI JAPAN/AUSTRALIA LIMITED

MIMI is a company formed co operatively by two major Japanese corporations, Mitsui and Mitsubishi. Its function is gas exploration and at present it is involved in a joint venture natural gas project off the northwest coast of Australia. It shares an interest in the Northwest Shelf Gas Project with Woodside Petroleum, British Petroleum, California Asiatic Oil Company, Shell and BHP Petroleum

MIMIは、日本の大手商社三井と三菱が、天然ガスを開発するため共同出資して設立した企業である。現在、オーストラリア大陸北西沖で天然ガスの共同開発に取り組んでいる。このプロジェクトには、ウッドサイド・ペトロリアム、ブリティッシュ・ペトロリアム、カリフォルニア・アジアティック・オイル・カンパニー、シェル、BHPペトロリアムが参加している。

AATEC AUSTRALIA PTY LTD

Aatec specialises in the manufacture of magnetic tape products. In particular, the company makes videotape, sound recording tape and floppy disks. The directors' approach to their business is uncompromising and, as a result, the quality of the product is excellent. Our visual identity program included the development of the logotype, a crisp, clean treatment of the company name, and their symbol which is based on the letter 'A' and emphasises the visual dimension of the business

アーテックは磁気テープ、特にビデオテープ、録音テープ、フロッピーディスクの専門メーカー。

経営陣は、「妥協せず」という方針を持っており、その結果、品質は卓越している。。われわれは、会社名をきびきびと明快なかたちにしたロゴ「Ａ」の字を基本にビジネスのひろがりを強調するシンボルマークを含むヴィジュアルアイデンティティプログラムを開発した。

Epitype is primarily a typesetting company and also a number of allied divisions. Epicolour is a facility for producing 'one off' printed items. Episcan is a colour and black and white separation facility for photo reproduction. These and other divisions the company has planned for the future all begin with the prefix "epi". It means "upon, at, in addition to, near, against" and is suggestive of an all encompassing role. Its versatility allows each division to stand alone yet clearly they are unified by this common element. Our task was to develop a visual identity program for Epitype and its divisions. Pictured are some of the posters produced for Epitype. One features all the typefaces available for headlines, another features body copy typefaces and the third is one of a series featuring information about typeface designers

84

エピタイプの中心は写植業だが、その他にも多くの関連産業を行っている。「エピカラー」はフィルムから焼き直しをおこす設備。エピタイプのこのような部門、機器。エピタイプのこのような部門は「エピ」という接頭辞を持つ。計画している部門はすべて「エピ」という接頭辞を持つ。これは「上に、そこに、加えて、近い、……に対して」その意味を持ち、オールラウンドな役割を示唆する。その自在さにより各部門は独立しながらも、「エピ」という共通要素により、明確に統合される。われわれへの依頼事項は、エピタイプの各部門のために、ヴィジュアルアイデンティティプログラムを開発することだった。ここにのせた三つのポスターはまず、見出しに使う書体を、次に本文の書体、そしてタイプフェイスデザイナーをそれぞれ主題にしている。

GOUDY NEVER GAUDY

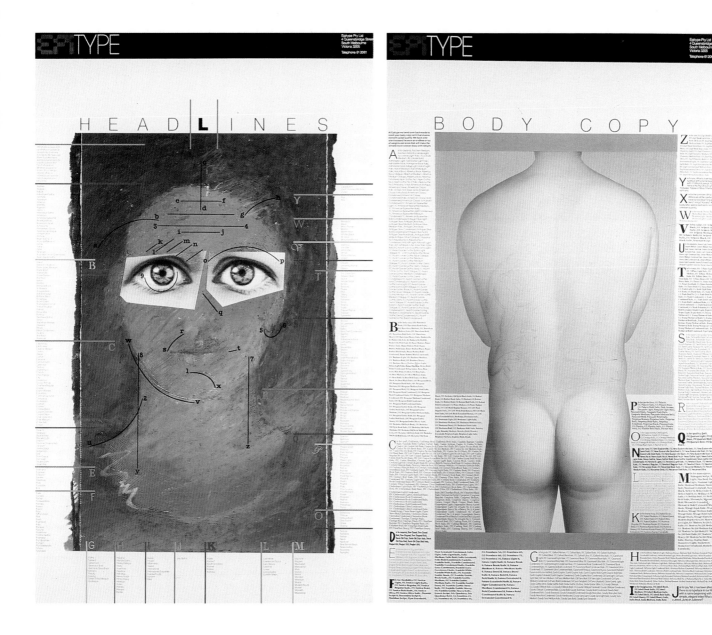

As a typehouse, Epitype regularly produces type manuals. These are designed to show the range of alphabets the company is able to set. To enhance the Epitype body type manual, we designed a special alphabet using 'bodies' of people and animals to create each letter. These were then used as index pages through the manual itself. The poster featuring Hermann Zapf is another in the series of typeface designers mentioned on the previous page

写植会社エピタイプは、定期的にいろいろな活字便覧を発行し、ここが現在持っているさまざまな字体をクライアントに知らせている。われわれはボディタイプ便覧のイメージを高めるため、人間と動物の体を使って特別のアルファベットをデザインし、索引ページに使用した。ハーマン・ザップをフィーチャーしたポスターは、前のページでふれたタイプフェイス・デザイナーシリーズのひとつである。

Epitype Pty Ltd
4–10 Queensbridge Street
South Melbourne
Victoria 3205
Telephone 614 2061
Facsimile 621 1734

If one quality characterises Hermann Zapf, it is zest. Today, he is nearly seventy but his enthusiasm for living and learning is ageless. During his lifetime so far, he has crafted more than one hundred and fifty typefaces including Palatino, Melior, Optima and Zapf itself, a range he designed in 1976. His skill as a calligrapher is renowned and he has written numerous books and articles about his interests.

Hermann Zapf was born in Nurnberg in Germany on November 8, 1918. As a child, he explored the woods bordering his town and, with his school friends, caught salamanders and gathered flowers and stones.

His interest in the 'black art' was not evident then although he was most impressed by the blackened hands of the local chimney-sweep. The idea of having such black hands without being scolded for it appealed to him enormously. At the age of four, he announced to his mother that he wished to be a chimney-sweep.

His marks for penmanship at school were not bad but not exceptional. His love for lettering did not find the space to be expressed until he was employed in his first job.

Hermann Zapf's father, a metal worker in a large automobile company, was crudely discharged in 1933, putting an end to any thoughts his son had entertained of studying electrical engineering at the technical school. Hermann Zapf had shown skill as a draftsman at school and his teachers advised him to look for an apprenticeship as a lithographer or colour etcher.

In March 1934 at the age of fifteen, he was employed at the Karl Ulrich & Co. printing plant, not as a platemaker but as a retoucher. His apprenticeship lasted four years and during that time he learnt a great deal. In 1935, he began to experiment with a broad-edged pen and discovered a sentiment expressed by the famous typographer, Rudolf Koch: 'The making of letters in every form is for me the purest and the greatest pleasure, and at many stages in my life it was to me what the song is to the singer, a picture to the painter, a shout to the elated, or a sigh to the oppressed – it was and is for me the most happy and perfect expression of my life.'

With his pocket money, Hermann Zapf bought Rudolf Koch's, 'Das Schreiben als Kunsterfertigkeit' (Lettering as a Craft) and Edward Johnston's 'Writing and Illuminating and Lettering.' With tireless zeal in his spare time he wrote pages and pages of letters and was always unhappy with his efforts 'until one day I discovered I had been holding my edged pen in a false position, whereupon things began to look up.'

His apprenticeship finished in 1938 and Hermann Zapf left his hometown and moved to Frankfurt. There he was introduced to the Stempel type-foundry and to a technique called punch-cutting. While extending his practical knowledge under the guidance of August Rosenberger, a master of this subtle craft, he designed his first alphabet, a German text face called Gilgengart.

The punch-cutting technique is painstakingly tedious and requires great patience. Originally, letters were cut by hand into hardened steel punches which were then stamped into little copper stumps to form moulds for the letters to be cast in lead.

To Hermann Zapf, there was a great sense of excited anticipation waiting for the first letters to be cast. 'They are seemingly transformed on the paper, now at last appearing in their native character to the designer. They seem either pure, graceful, true of image, quite as he conceived them.' On the other hand, they could be 'Knavishly grinning, awry, as if out of insolence ready to fall on their faces, or too gally hop-dancing on the line, wilful, unregarding of their neighbours.'

In 1939 the war started. Before Hermann Zapf was conscripted he designed the lettering book 'Feder und Stichel,' featuring 25 alphabets and calligraphic pages. He was not able to finish it until 1941 and in those two years his mentor, August Rosenberger, cut all the plates by hand with an extraordinary amount of care and patience in between trips to the air-raid shelter.

Perhaps it was at this time that Hermann Zapf crystallised his thoughts about calligraphy, although he did not actually commit them to paper until years later: 'Calligraphy is a peaceful and noble art, practised by well-educated human beings who do their work with full commitment, and intense concentration. For we want to put into our letters a little of our own feelings, of our own personality and mood. The letters should have grace and beauty about them.

As a soldier, Hermann Zapf was assigned to an administrative position in southern France. Taking advantage of every spare minute, he collected stag beetles and butterflies from the nearby acacia forests because he needed them as models for his alphabet, Blumen – ABC.

After the war, he returned to the Stempel type-foundry where he was appointed artistic director. He also accepted a position as lettering instructor at the same technical school at which Rudolf Koch had taught. Hermann Zapf discovered the following direct and rather terse quotation from the philosopher, Gottfried Wilhelm Leibniz: 'The man who has taught the ABC to his pupils has accomplished a greater deed than a general who has won a battle.' Of it, he said: 'This was a comment upon teaching in general; yet even 200 years after the great philosopher's death such views have yet to find universal acceptance.'

From 1946 onwards, Hermann Zapf worked steadily, designing typefaces in earnest. Palatino was produced almost immediately. By 1950, it was destined for extension into a type family. To date, there are over a dozen different founts including the Linotype Palatino Italic and a narrower italic for hand-setting.

At the same time, Hermann Zapf continued his inscriptional studies. He made an important trip to Italy in 1950 to seek out Roman inscriptions in Florence, Pisa and Rome. These were studies which were to greatly influence his later work.

'Every lover of beautiful letter forms will understand how transported I was by the inscription on the Trajan Column, erected in the Foro Traiano, Rome, in 114AD.' In fact, Hermann Zapf viewed typefaces as personalities in their own right. The 'slender' Michelangelo, the 'powerful' Sistina, the various members of the Palatino family, Melior and the infamous Optima were the next alphabets to take shape in the ensuing few years.

In 1957, Hermann Zapf resigned from his position with the Stempel type-foundry to concentrate on his typography and book design. His 'Manuale Typographicum' had first appeared in 1954. A majestic work, it contained texts concerning type and typography in sixteen different languages. Now he was free to concentrate on the second volume.

He did not use only his own typefaces when designing books

'No calligrapher pollutes rivers with his ink, or poisons the air we breathe. Calligraphy makes no noise. We don't fight with arms or our pens, but sometimes we do want to convince with a handwritten message of special importance in which we believe.'

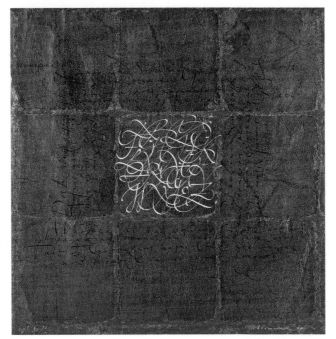

ZAPF WITH ZEST

typographically. He often used the work of others he admired. To explain his feelings, he cites the tale of Brahms who was asked how he liked the Kaiser Waltz of Johann Strauss. Brahms replied: 'Marvellous! Too bad it's not mine!'

'Something of the sort happens to me when I look at Roger Excotton's Mistral type, or the Diotima along with its lovely italic by Gudrun Zapf-von Hesse...But this latter 'competitor' has now become less dangerous, for I have married her.' Gudrun Zapf-von Hesse is, like her husband, an accomplished calligrapher and type designer.

Hermann Zapf's approach to type design has always been practical. A type contrived for newspaper text would hardly be suited to a volume of lyric verses.

Consequently a typeface needed a series of considerations, trials and comparisons, often taking years before a design could be submitted for approval. He considered typographers who did not use this approach to be 'typographic mayflies.'

From 1960 onwards, printing methods had advanced considerably into the technical and electronic age. Photocomposition now influences the letterforms in the same way as type casting did with the calligraphy of the mediaeval monks.

Hunt Roman was designed in 1961. The typeface had been commissioned by the Carnegie Institute of Technology in Pittsburgh, USA, for the Hunt Botanical Library. It took several months to produce the first sketches of the complete alphabet and meet Hermann Zapf's own aim of producing a face that was not a revival but rather a type of the time.

'The designer of a new typeface has a responsibility, not only to the past masters of type design but also to the future.'

All his work since then has rather reflected this view. In particular the typeface range that bears his name, Zapf, and specialist typefaces, like AMS – Euler, an alphabet commissioned by the Department of Computer Science at Stanford University for the American Mathematical Society. He has not fallen behind but has continued to experiment with letter forms.

Hermann Zapf is often asked how he manages all the various tasks in which he is continually engaged. His answer is the two ideal places in which he works. One is an old watch tower in Dreieichenhaln (Three Oaks Grove) near Frankfurt, built in 1460 when Gutenberg was printing the Catholicon in a small village 40 kilometres away; and his summer place in Cervo, on the Riviera del Fiori between Genoa and Nice, facing the Mediterranean.

'Two places without telephones, two splendid refuges for work. The main question is time, but I think it is much more important how to organise the amount of time given to you within the span of your lifetime. If only we knew our allotted span of days!'

Zest for life is a quality for which Hermann Zapf will be remembered. It is as powerful an expression of his being as are all the typefaces he has designed. He is a truly creative man. He is forever hopeful and optimistic about the future and never satisfied with his past performances.

'And if letters, 'our letters,' were to help only once to lessen hatred and mistrust among peoples; if the many printed reports were to make a dweller on this earth into the happiest being; if printed letters might once rout a calumny with truth, or through a consoling book reconcile a single human being with his fellow creatures; then shall we be immune against all the glitter of riches, the lust for power and idle fame, which seduce so many. If the letters daily produced by millions in the printing presses were to be used for only one good purpose every day, then – despite all abuse – all the pains we have taken with their creation will have been rewarded.'

As design consultants to the leading cigarette manufacturer, Philip Morris, we develop packaging designs for their brands which are marketed in Australia, Singapore, Malaysia, China, Hong Kong, Korea, Pakistan, Japan, India and the Philippines. The two brands shown on this page are marketed in Australia. Cigarette brands are produced for quite specific segments of the smoking market and the design for each brand must clearly reflect its marketing strategy

大手煙草メーカー、フィリップ・モリスのデザインコンサルタントとして、われわれはオーストラリア、シンガポール、マレーシア、中国、香港、韓国、パキスタン、日本、インド、フィリピンで販売されるブランドのパッケージを作った。ここにのせた二つのブランドはオーストラリア向け。煙草のブランドは市場の中でもかなりはっきりした部分に向けて販売されるもので、一つ一つのブランドはそのマーケティング戦略を忠実に反映していなくてはならない。

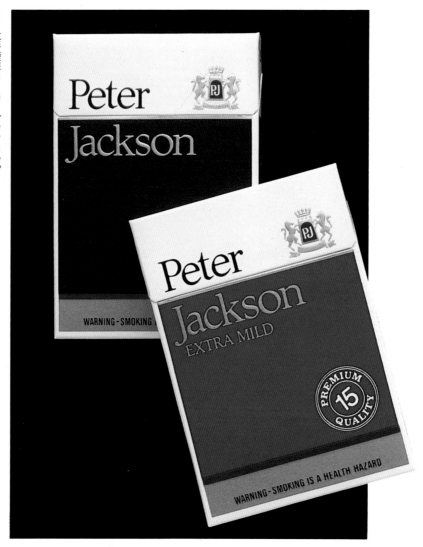

PHILIP MORRIS ASIA-PACIFIC INC

K2 and Black and White are Philip Morris brands marketed in Pakistan. K2 is a traditional cigarette for which we modernised the packaging. Black and White is a prestige cigarette and we developed a pack to reflect this image. Also shown is the pack we designed for Abdullah, a popular brand marketed in Hong Kong and China

「K2」と「ブラック・アンド・ホワイト」はフィリップ・モリスのパキスタン向けブランド。「K2」は昔からのタバコで、パッケージを現代的なものにした。「ブラック・アンド・ホワイト」は最高級タバコのイメージを反映するパッケージをデザインした。もう一つは香港と中国市場に出される一般向けの「アブダラー」のパッケージである。

S C JOHNSON & SON PTY LTD

In the competitive field of air freshener products, S C Johnson is market leader.
When they introduced different fragrances into their Open Air range of products, our task was to design the packs with a strong visual similarity and, at the same time, show each fragrance clearly. Fragrance is a major factor in the decision to purchase off the shelf products in this category. The images we chose to depict the range of frangrances have a fresh, evocative quality. The design for the Smoke Away packaging is also aimed at capturing impulse purchases and deliberately makes an overt statement about the product benefit

競争の激しいエアフレッシュナー業界にあって、S・C・ジョンスンはマーケットリーダーである。オープンエアーシリーズに新たな香りを加えて発表しようとしたS・C・ジョンスンの意向は、シリーズの前のパッケージデザインと視覚的同質性を保ちながらも、その香りの差異をはっきりと示すパッケージデザインをというものだった。消費者が、スーパーマーケットの棚の上にならんだこの種の商品を手にとってカゴに入れるかどうかを決める大きな要因は、その香りだからである。われわれは、その香りがいずれも新鮮な、しかも喚起的な香りであることをうまく表現するイメージを選んだ。「スモークアウェイ」のパッケージもまた買う人の衝動をうまくつかむことをめざして、この商品のもつ価値をずばりと伝えるようにした。

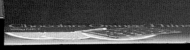

RED TULIP CHOCOLATES PTY LTD

Red Tulip is a leading confectionery manufacturer and produces, amongst other fine products, a range of quality chocolates. Confectionery is more often than not an impulse purchase. The packaging design plays a vital role in influencing the decision of the purchaser. It must not only present a description of the contents but also general appetite appeal and convey an impression of the product which accurately reflects its quality and its price. In each of the packs shown, illustrative techniques communicate the stylish, sophisticated personality of the product inside

レッドチューリップは、高級チョコレート各種などを生産販売する大手製菓会社。菓子はしばしば衝動買いする商品であるから、パッケージデザインは購買の決定を左右するきわめて大切な要因である。内容をきちんと示すだけでなく、食指をそそるアピールを持ち、品質と価格を正確に反映しているという印象を与えねばならない。ここにあげたそれぞれのパッケージイラストレーションのテクニックは、中の製品の洗練された上品さを伝えている。

Beecham is a large and aggressive marketer of a variety of products including toiletries and beauty aids. The packaging designs shown were developed to update the identity of this range of anti-perspirant spray deodorants. This exercise exemplified the need for well established products to be reviewed within their own category in order to maintain a viable and competitive image

ビーチャムはトイレタリーや化粧品の先駆的な大手メーカー。このパッケージデザインは、発汗をおさえるスプレー式デオドラントシリーズのアイデンティティを、現代的な感覚に合わせるように作ったもの。競争力がありまた息が長いというイメージを維持するために、それまでによく知られた製品を、そのカテゴリーを変えずにみなおす必要があるという一つの例である。

WEAVER AND LOCK

The Western Australian based company, Weaver and Lock, manufacture and market a range of soft drinks. We developed an identity program for the company which was featured on stationery items, vehicles and signage. We were also asked to redesign the packaging for their ranges of children's soft drinks, adult mixers, mineral waters, cordials and fruit juice drinks.

ウィーヴァー・アンド・ロックは西オーストラリア州に本社を持つソフトドリンクメーカー。アイデンティティプログラムは、事務用品、車輛、サイニッジに使われている。また、子供向けのソフトドリンク、大人向けのトニックウォーターなどのミクサー、ミネラルウォーター、清涼飲料水、フルーツジュースドリンク等のパッケージもデザインし直した。

Decoré, marketed by Reckitts Toiletries International, is the leading brand of haircare products in Australia. The company sells colourants, shampoos, conditioners and allied products through pharmacies and supermarkets. Decoré must compete for attention in supermarkets and pharmacies, both highly competitive environments where impact on the shelf is vital. We were appointed to redesign the packaging for the entire product range

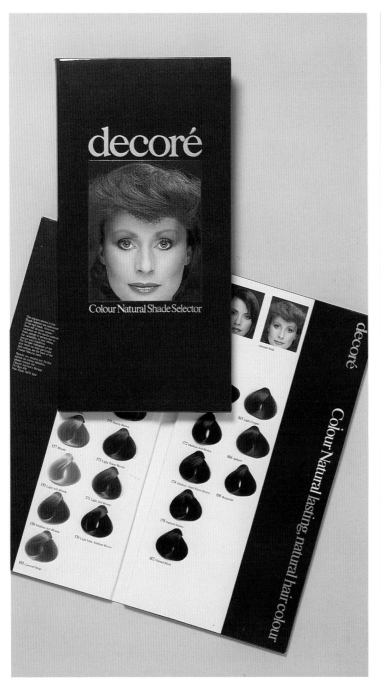

レキッツ・トイレトリーズ・インターナショナルの「デコレ」シリーズは、オーストラリア市場屈指のヘアケア製品。ヘアカラー、シャンプー、コンディショナーなどを全国の薬局やスーパーマーケットで販売している。「デコレ」は、激しい競争の中で、消費者の注意をひきつけなくてはならないため、デザイン的には商品棚の上でいかに強いインパクトを与えるかが最も大切である。

RECKITTS TOILETRIES INTERNATIONAL

We developed a disciplined design style to maintain a strong family image while allowing the different Decoré product groups, each designed with a strong individual theme, to tell their own story

われわれはシリーズ全部のパッケージをまかされ、きちんとしたスタイルで家庭的なイメージを強く打ち出す一方、「デコレ」のそれぞれの部門が自ら語りかけるようにした。

設立当初のヴェガ・プレスは野心を持った小さな印刷所であり、経営陣はカラー印刷の質の追求という姿勢を貫きながらも、ヴェガ・プレスを大手の印刷所に仕立て上げることをねらっていた。

われわれはまず、ヴェガ・プレスの力量について認識を深めさせるためのダイレクトメールキャンペーンに参加し、精妙な印刷技術を必要とする複雑な作品のシリーズを作成した。ヴェガ・プレスはこの挑戦に応じ、作品の多くはコレクターズ・アイテムとなった。封筒入り、一六頁のイラストブック「ブルー・ジョークス」はその第一作である。その後、一枚一枚に黄色のイラストのついたトランプセット「イエローズ」が続いた。それからも数多くの作品を手がけたがその中にいくつかカレンダーもある。ここにのせたのは、「ヴァイオレット」シリーズから二種と、「ピンクの象とおかしな動物たち」シリーズから一枚である。

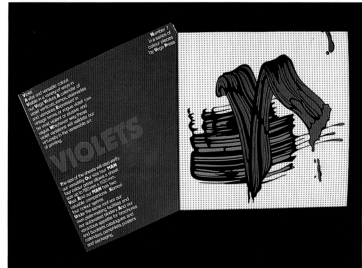

VEGA PRESS PTY LTD

When Vega Press was first established, it was a small printery with an aggressive intention. The company's strength lay in the directors' commitment to quality colour printing and their aim was to make Vega Press a major supplier. We were first commissioned to produce a direct mail campaign to create awareness of their capabilities. Consequently, we developed a series of complex pieces which demanded nothing less than superb printing. Vega rose to the challenge and many of the pieces are now collectors' items. Vega's Blue Jokes, a 16 page illustrated book in its own envelope, was the very first piece in the promotional campaign. Vega's Yellows followed, a complete pack of playing cards, each containing an illustrated item of interest about the colour yellow. Among the many pieces we continued to produce have been several calendars. Shown is the packaging and two of the sheets from Vega's Violets, and one of the sheets from Vega's Pink Elephants and Other Curious Creatures.

VEGA PRESS PTY LTD

The program eventually developed into a series of illustrated limited edition posters, each of which were signed by the artist, designers, colour separator and printer.
The company's aim has now largely been realised and our long association has been an excellent example of how design can make a significant contribution to a company's image power. Vega's visual identity clearly reflects the impression they want to give.
Their ability to supply quality colour printing is obvious

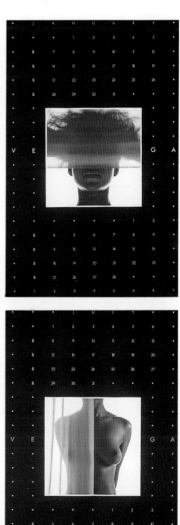

MARCH

S					1	2
S	4	5	6	7	8	9
S	11	12	13	14	15	16
S	18	19	20	21	22	23
S	25	26	27	28	29	30

V E   G A

	1	2	3	4	5	6
S	8	9	10	11	12	13
S	15	16	17	18	19	20
S	22	23	24	25	26	27
S	29	30				

APRIL

August   2 3 4 5 6 7 9 10 11 12 13 14 16 17 18 19 20 21 23 24 25 26 27 28 30 31

VEGA PRESS PTY LTD

A number of the items we produced for Vega Press have been calendars in the form of photographic essays. As you can see here with Vega's Blackbirds calendar, they not only provided an opportunity for imaginative photography but also put to the test Vega's printing capabilities.

Vega's Blackbirds — 1976 — December

Vega's Blackbirds — 1977 — February

Vega's Blackbirds — 1977 — April

Vega's Blackbirds — 1977 — June

われわれは、ヴェガ・プレスのために写文集のかたちをとったカレンダーをかなり作ってきた。どれもこのページのブラックバード・カレンダーでわかるように、想像力ゆたかな写真をみせるだけでなく、ヴェガ・プレスの印刷能力を証明するものでもある。

プログラムは最終的には、一枚一枚がアーティスト、デザイナー、カラーセパレイター、印刷会社のサイン入り限定版イラストポスターへと発展した。ヴェガ・プレスの野心は大方達成され、われわれとヴェガ・プレスとの長期にわたる友交関係は、デザインが企業のイメージパワーにいかに大きく貢献するかの、すぐれた例証となったヴェガ・プレスのヴィジュアルアイデンティティは彼等が与えたいと思った印象をはっきりと伝え、質の高いカラー印刷能力が明瞭に示されている。

AUSTRALIA POST

Postpak and Express Courier are two of several services introduced by Australia Post to ensure mail is delivered as quickly and safely as possible. Postpak is a range of protective mailing tubes and cartons for odd shaped and fragile items. Express Courier is a high speed messenger service that delivers items quickly, locally. Pictured are the two logotypes, designed to communicate the most important benefit of each service

「ポストパック」と「エクスプレス・クーリエ」は、オーストラリアポストが迅速かつ安全に郵便物を配達するために始めたサービスのうちの二つ。「ポストパック」は非定型、あるいはこわれやすいものを郵送するための円筒とカートンの容器であり、「エクスプレス・クーリエ」は、各地区で迅速に郵便物を配達するサービスである。ここにのせたロゴは、それぞれのサービスの最も重要な役割を伝えるためにデザインされた。

COLLIE AND COMPANY PTY LTD

Collie and Company have been supplying inks and related products to the graphic arts industry for many years. Their market extends across Australia to South East Asia. The corporate image program we designed for them included a fresh new symbol and logotype imprinted on stationery, packaging, promotional items and signage for vehicles and buildings. Pictured are the symbol and logotype on a delivery van, and a printed piece announcing the change of name and style. Below is the symbol as it was designed, in striking contrasting colours and flexible form evolving from the letter C

コリー・アンド・カンパニーは、長年にわたりインクおよびその関連商品をグラフィックアート業界に供給し、その市場はオーストラリアはもとより、東南アジアにまでひろがっている。われわれが作ったコーポレイトイメージプログラムの中には、新しいシンボルやロゴが印刷された便せん、ボールペンなどの文具、パッケージ、あるいは建物の看板等が含まれるパンフレット、この写真は、配達バンにつけたシンボルとロゴ、それに名称とスタイルの変更を知らせるパンフレットである。下段のシンボルマークは、Cという文字からあざやかなコントラストの色を使って、Cという文字から柔軟なかたちにした。

a change
of name

and a change
of style for
collies

leaders in
the graphic
arts

The National University Hospital is one of the main hospitals in Singapore. A teaching and private care institution, it is adjacent to the university. The cross was developed as a mark because it traditionally represents medical help. Also, it was possible to endow it with a strong human feeling to support the hospital's philosophy. The symbol became the focus of a visual identity program and was used extensively on a range of items including ambulances

国立大学病院はシンガポールの大病院。大学に隣接し、教育と治療が行なわれている。
十字は伝統的に医療のシンボルであり、ここでもそれを用いて、病院の理念である力強い人間的な感情を加味した。
このシンボルマークはヴィジュアルアイデンティティプログラムの焦点となり、救急車などに巾広くつけられている。

マリーナ・スクエアは、シンガポール有数の土地開発事業である。ホテル三つ、小売店二五〇、デパート四、映画館三、巨大な地下駐車場一つを持ち、内外の企業に対し、賃貸スペースを提供している。ここでとりあげた二つのパンフレットの表紙は、このコンプレックスの雰囲気と、海辺という場所を効果的に伝えている。また水のあしらいとレタリングで、世界有数のビジネスセンターであり中継貿易基地としてのシンガポールとの関連を持たせ、機能しているシンガポールとの関連を持たせ、イメージを高めている。パンフレットの一つは小売店用の貸ビルについて利点をくわしく述べ、もう一つはシンガポールの人口、観光産業、通貨、それにマーケティングの有望性について述べている。

Marina Square is a major Singapore Land development. Its three hotels, 250 retail stores, 4 department stores, 3 cinemas and a vast underground carpark offered numerous leasing opportunities for local and overseas companies. The covers of the two books shown suit the mood of the complex and effectively communicate its position by the sea. Further, the use of water and the treatment of the lettering elevate the property in terms of its relationship to Singapore, one of the major business and stopover centres in the world. One book describes the building in detail and the opportunities it offers to retail traders. The other provides information about Singapore the country, its population, tourist trade, currency and potential marketing opportunities

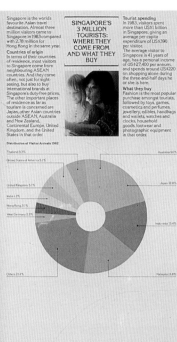

The Marina Mandarin is an imposing international hotel complex in Singapore.
The comprehensive identity program was developed around the corporate symbol,
a decorative 'M' repeated upside down, not only to symbolise the hotel name but
also to suggest a reflection in water, a theme that locates the hotel on the water's edge.
Each of the hotel's facilities required an individual identity and we developed these for
the discotheque, brasserie, Italian restaurant, French restaurant, Chinese restaurant,
English 'pub,' poolside dining area, banquet rooms and health club.

114

マリーナ・マンダリンはシンガポールの誇る国際ホテルコンプレックスである。広範なヴィジュアルアイデンティティプログラムは装飾的な上下対称の二つの「M」のシンボルマークを基本としている。このシンボルは、ホテルの名前を象徴するだけでなく、水面に立つホテルが水面に映りこんでいる状態をも暗示する。ホテルの各設備にそれぞれのアイデンティティが必要だったので、われわれは、ディスコ、ブラスリー、イタリアンレストラン、フレンチレストラン、チャイニーズレストラン、イギリスの「パブ」、プールサイドのダイニング・エリア、バンケットルーム、そしてヘルスクラブのためにアイデンティティをつくった。

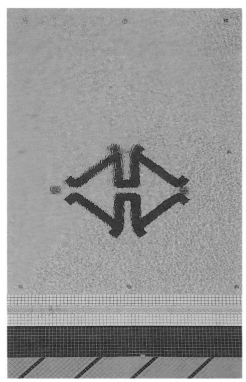

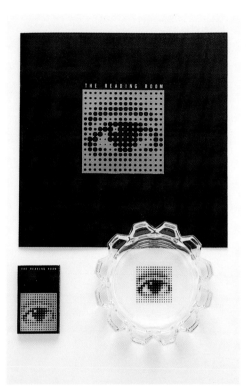

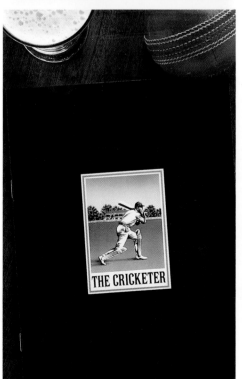

AAV AUSTRALIA PTY LTD

AAV Australia offers one of the largest recording facilities for broadcast in Australia.
The company is one of the Selcom Group, all of which offer allied audio visual services.
A visual identity program was required not only to clearly identify each company but
to link each one with a common graphic theme. The corporate logotype for AAV appears
on stationery, signage, videotapes, audiotapes, vehicles and equipment

ＡＡＶオーストラリアは、
放送用録音設備の大手。
セルコムグループの一員であり、
視聴覚関連では提携して
活動する。ヴィジュアル
アイデンティティプログラムは、
各会社の存在を明瞭に伝える
だけでなく、共通のグラフィック
テーマでそれぞれを結びつけるものを
作らなくてはならなかった。
ＡＡＶのコーポレイトロゴは
事務用品、看板、ビデオテープ、
オーディオテープ、自動車、
それに録音設備につけられている。

AAV Australia

VICTORIA'S 150TH ANNIVERSARY

To promote the 150th anniversary of Victoria, a state in south-east Australia, a series of posters were developed as part of the official activities. Their function was to suggest a variety of inspirational ideas for further visual pieces, such as banners and mobiles, which could be produced by schools, community groups and individuals as their contribution to the anniversary festivities. The posters were also displayed in their own right and helped to achieve the 150th Anniversary Committee's aim which was to 'paint the state with a giant splash of colour, an innovative and interesting approach to mark such an historic occasion

The street banners shown are a real example of the suggestions implicit in the series of motivational posters produced. Based on the triangle theme, the banners were the official form of decoration used by the City of Melbourne for the duration of Victoria's 150th celebrations. They were also made available for use throughout Victoria's cities and towns

オーストラリア南東部、ヴィクトリア州の一五〇周年をプロモートする公的な活動の一部として、ポスターシリーズを作った。これは、学校、コミュニティグループ、個人が記念祝典行事のために作るのぼりや、市電につけるポスターなどの視覚的宣伝物に、インスピレーションを与える役割をになっていた。このポスターはその他、一五〇周年委員会の「大きな色ののぼとばしりで州を飾る」という、革新的で興味深い構想に沿って、あちこちに貼り出された。

ここで紹介した街頭ののぼりは、ポスターシリーズが示唆したテーマが実現した一例。三角形のテーマののぼりは、ヴィクトリア州一五〇周年祝典のテーマに基いた期間中メルボルン市が公式に採用したが、同州の他の都市や町でも使われた。

ULTIMATE FUNDS LIMITED

Ultimate Funds is an investment company established to offer its customers four investment funds, each paying a high fluctuating rate of interest. The company has impeccable credentials and an excellent track record and is supported by some very influential people in the business world. We developed a visual identity program to reinforce their credibility and to demonstrate their dynamism and innovative approach to investment

アルティミット・ファンズは利率の高い投資ファンドを提供する投資会社。絶大の信用と優秀な実績を持ち、財界に強い影響力を持つ人々から支持を得ている。われわれはその信用をさらに強化し、投資に対する精力的かつ革新的な姿勢を示すための、ヴィジュアルアイデンティティプログラムをつくった。

NOLA CHARLES

Nola Charles is an interior designer whose work is strongly identified by the imaginative use of bold colours and geometric shapes. Her visual identity program features an interpretation of her initials to demonstrate her style and her signature further reinforces her individuality. Her philosophy in relation to her work is made very clear. Pictured is her business card and the cover of her presentation folder

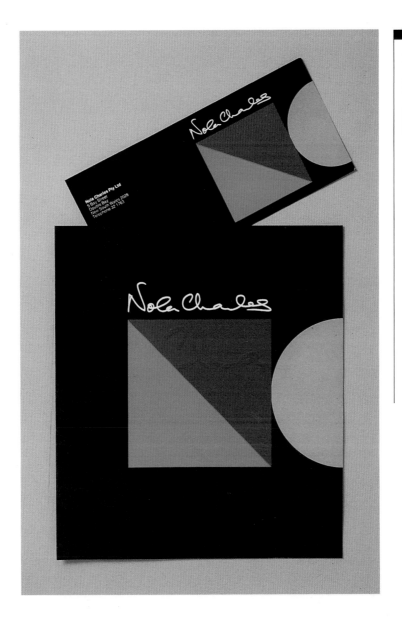

ノーラ・チャールズのインテリア
デザインは、その大胆な色づかいと、
想像力に富む幾何学模様で
よく知られている。
彼女のイニシャルを
翻案し、デザインスタイルと
サインを強調したヴィジュアル
アイデンティティプログラムは、
このデザイナーの個性を
よくあらわしている。
彼女の仕事に対する姿勢は
非常に明解である。写真は
名刺と、プレゼンテーション
フォルダーの表紙。

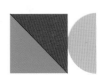

Glass is an excellent medium to show off products that are rich in colour and texture, like jam. Here, the colour of the fruit was inspiration for the packaging designs. This popular brand of conserves and marmalade has a 'family' look across all of the products. Each can be quickly and easily identified. The labels are clearly branded, they maximise the products' own visual appeal and the legal requirements, including ingredients and the bar code, have been neatly and inconspicuously placed around the sides of the jar. The lids of the jars were once white, causing them to be unnecessarily dominant. Now the lids are in complementary colours and attention is immediately drawn to the brand name and the contents

122

ガラスは、ジャムのような美しい色や質感を持つ商品をはっきりみせる、すばらしい材料である。ここでは、果物の色がパッケージデザインのインスピレーションとなった。ヘンリー・ジョーンズはジャムとマーマレードの人気ブランドで、全商品を通じて「家庭的」な顔を持ち、それぞれの製品は色などから簡単に見分けがつくようになっている。ラベルははっきりとブランドを示しており、商品自身の視覚的な訴えかけを最大限に生かし、法律による原材料名表示やバーコードは、ビンの側面にきちんと目ざわりにならないようにつけられている。以前のフタは白くて目立ちすぎたが、それをあらため、内容物の色の補色にして、消費者の目がすぐにブランドネームと内容物にゆくようにしている。

DURACELL BATTERIES AUSTRALIA PTY LTD

There are times when the inherent design qualities of a product do more to influence opinion than any amount of promotion. It needs little help to communicate its qualities. The Duracell range of torches is permanently displayed in the Museum of Modern Art in New York. It has also won several international industrial design awards. In some respects, it is a challenge to design a package that allows a product to speak for itself. It is necessary to devise a method of displaying it without interrupting its image. In this case, blister packages answered the problem efficiently. Simple graphics were added merely to introduce each product

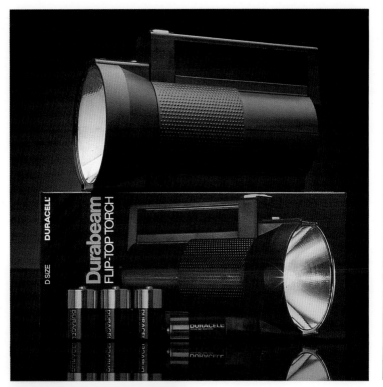

ある商品特有のデザインが、他のどんなプロモーションより購買者に影響を与える場合がある。そうしたデザインは、殆どそれだけで、商品の品質をも語ってしまう。デュラセルの懐中電灯シリーズはニューヨーク近代美術館に常設展示されているし、国際産業デザイン賞もいくつか受けている。商品自体が語り出すようなパッケージデザインをすることはそういう意味で難しいが、やりがいもある。そのイメージの邪魔をせずにみせる方式を作り出す必要があるわけである。ここではブリスターパッケージ（ボール紙を背に製合品を入れる商品のかたちに成型をし、透明プラスチックをかぶせたもの）がこの問題を明快に解決した。これからあとはシンプルなデザインをつけて、それぞれの商品を紹介するだけでよかったのである。

SAMPLE INDUSTRIES PTY LTD

Sample Industries manufacture the GJ Works range of automotive products.
The packaging has been designed within a graphic system to communicate a powerful,
consistent visual identity. This system has the flexibility to be interpreted across a broad
range of package shapes and sizes. This bold approach creates instant brand
identification, as well as identifying individual products, at a point of sale level.
The packages ranged in size from small 25mL containers to large 44 gallon drums

BEECHAM (AUSTRALIA) PTY LTD

Passiona has long been established in Australia. It is well known and well liked yet in an increasingly competitive market, it needed an aggressive new image. We retained the colour scheme and added new life and strength to the package design. At once, it became a simpler, more powerful and easily identifiable image reflecting the tropical, summery attributes inherent in the product

「パッショーナ」は、オーストラリア市場で長く安定した地位を占め、よく知られ、よい評判を得ている。しかし、市場競争が激しくなったため、もっと強くはたらきかける新しいイメージが必要となった。われわれは色彩設計はそのままにし、パッケージデザインに新しい生命を吹き込み、強さを与えた。すると、この製品に固有な熱帯の夏の感じを反映したイメージ、もっと力強い、人をひきつけるイメージが生まれたのである。

サンプル・インダストリーズは、自動車用各種オイルなどの「GJワックス」シリーズを製造する。パッケージは強力で一貫したヴィジュアルアイデンティティを伝えるシステムのひとつとしてデザインされた。このシステムは、パッケージの形状やサイズに応じて、柔軟に用いられている。大胆なやり方だが、ひとめ見てそのブランドだとわかる。パッケージは、小は二五ミリリットルから大は四四ガロン入りドラムカンまで。

H J HEINZ COMPANY AUSTRALIA LIMITED

Heinz produces a vast range of canned and bottled food products. Pictured are some examples of our packaging designs for their salads and tomato products. 'Big Red', a promotional name coined initially for their tomato soup, has now become the 'personality' for their entire range of tomato products including juice, whole peeled tomatoes, sauce and soups. Heinz has a powerful presence in retail food outlets and to effectively design labels for its products, it is important not only to quickly convey the brand and contents but to sustain a favourable image of the company too

ハインツはカンづめ、ビンづめ食品を巾広く製造する。ここにのせたのは、サラダとトマトのパッケージ。「ビッグレッド」ははじめはトマトケチャップの販売促進のためにつくられた言葉だったが、今はジュース、ピューレー、丸むきトマト、ケチャップ、スープなどすべてのトマト製品の「パーソナリティ」となった。ハインツは食品業界では大手であり、効果的なラベルをデザインするためには、ブランドと内容をすみやかに伝えるだけでなく、ハインツのよいイメージを保つことが大切だった。

Leo Buring has maintained a prominent position in Australia's winemaking history since the 1930s. In 1962, the company became part of the giant Lindemans Wines group. We have had a long association with Leo Buring and, over the years, have produced many label designs for their fine wines. Those shown reflect the confidence and sophistication with which the company's winemakers are associated

リオ・ビュアリングはオーストラリアのワイン醸造史の上で、一九三〇年代以来卓越した地位を占めてきた。一九六二年には、大手ワインメーカーのリンデマン・ワインズ・グループの一員となった。われわれはリオ・ビュアリングと長いつきあいがあり、彼等の素晴しいワインのラベルをデザインしてきた。このラベルは、リオ・ビュアリングのワインメーカーたちの自信と洗練度を反映している。

132

H B R

DEAN

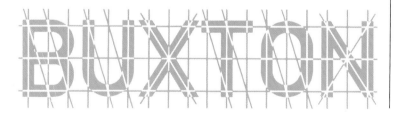

BUXTON

リナ・ガンは、グラフィックデザインおよび広告業に巾広い経験を持つイラストレーター。ヴィジュアルアイデンティティプログラムをつくる際、彼女独特のスタイルをはっきり示すイラストを事務用品につけ、パーソナリティを出すよう提案した。ここにのせたデザインは、多くのせた事務用品に使われている。

シンボルマーク。（上から下へ）店舗など商業インテリアデザインコンサルタント会社、HBR・デザイングループ。輸入コンサルタント会社、D・J・ディーン・エンタープライジス。家庭防犯設備会社、バクストン・セキュリティ。

Lena Gan is an illustrator with a wide range of experience in the graphic design and advertising industries. When we designed her visual identity program, we suggested she personalise her stationery with her own illustrations of relevant images to demonstrate her particular style. The design shown appeared on a range of stationery items

LENA GAN

8/43 ARMADALE STREET, ARMADALE, VICTORIA 3143, AUSTRALIA, TELEPHONE 500 0710

The Herald is one of the major daily newspapers in Australia. Recently the company decided to update its image. We were asked to redesign the editorial space within the newspaper and to design the covers for its new daily magazine supplements. The masthead, bylines and editorial typography were progressively revised to project an overall contemporary style.

オーストラリアの有力日刊紙「ヘラルド」は、イメージアップのため、紙面のデザインを変え、新しいマガジンタイプの付録をつけた。われわれは第一面の氏名欄、署名欄、それに社説欄のデザインを一新し、全体に現代的なスタイルの感じを出した。またマガジンタイプの付録の表紙もデザインした。

When a company manufacturing and retailing a range of fine quality furniture was restructured and relaunched, we were asked to develop a name and an identity to reflect the company's future direction. The name and logotype emphasise the company's commitment to innovation in the design and style of the furniture produced. The visual identity program was implemented through signage, stationery and point of sale items

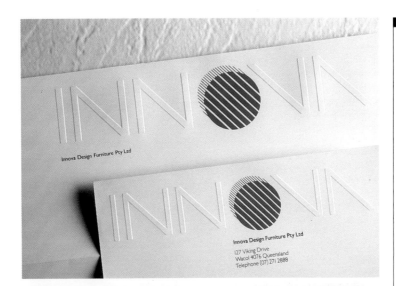

イノーヴァは、高級家具
製造販売会社が機構を改革し、
再出発して生まれた
会社である。われわれは
新会社の将来の方向を
反映する名称を考え、
アイデンティティを開発した。
その名称とロゴは、家具の
デザイン、およびスタイルの
革新に取り組む姿勢を
強調している。ヴィジュアル
アイデンティティプログラムは、
看板、事務用品、
POSアイテムに適用されている。

SUSSAN CORPORATION (AUSTRALIA) LIMITED

Sussans Secret is a division of the Sussan Corporation. It is a separate chain of stores selling lingerie and other personal attire for women. The visual identity program reflects a soft, feminine elegance and is an accurate representation of the company's personality

ススン・シークレットはススサン・コーポレイションの一部門。ランジェリー、インナーなどを扱うチェーンストアである。ヴィジュアルアイデンティティプログラムは、やわらかい、女性的なエレガンスをテーマにススサン・コーポレイションのコーポレイションの性格を正確に表現した。

シェリダンは、シーツその他のベッドルーム製品市場において、オーストラリア最大のシェアを持つ企業で、最近バスルーム製品部門を設立した。そのためわれわれは、シェリダンのロゴとうまく合うシンボルマークを作り、彼等のインテリアデザインに対する造詣の深さと、現代的な色使いに対する理解度とを反映させた。このページの作品はシェリダンが製造するバスマット、フェイスウォッシャー、トイレシートカバー、タオル、バスシート、シャワーカーテンなどのそれぞれのシリーズのために、われわれが開発したヴィジュアルアイデンティティプログラムの一部である。われわれはラベルをデザインし、アップリケシリーズに、他の商品に採用したような、おちついたパッケージを考案するよう依頼された。

SHERIDAN TEXTILES

Sheridan dominate the market in sheets and other bedroom products in
Australia. Recently, the company created a division to market products for the bathroom.
We developed a symbol, compatible with their existing logotype, that was designed
to reflect their understanding of interior design and appreciation of contemporary colours.
This was included in the identity programs we developed for each range the company
produced. There were bathmats, face washers, toilet seat covers, towels, bath sheets and
shower curtains. Our task was to design labels and, in the case of the Applique range,
unobtrusive packaging as well as some point of sale items

Magna Charta creates maps of major cities throughout the world and offers advertising space on the reverse side of each map to hotels, restaurants, airlines and other relevant companies. The maps are distributed free to tourists. We developed an identity program for Magna Charta and also provided them with a flexible format in which to arrange the advertising space.

138

マグナ・カルタは、世界の主要都市で旅行者に無料で配る地図を作成する。その地図の裏には、ホテル、レストラン、航空会社のリストや旅行関係の広告をのせている。われわれは、アイデンティティプログラムの開発の他、広告スペースを考えて柔軟なレイアウト構成を行なった。

ADDIT AUSTRALIA PTY LTD

Addit is a company established to devise and market add on products or peripheral devices for the computer industry. The name was chosen to reflect the company's purpose. It is crisp, easy to remember and is reinforced by the symbol, an abstract "plus" sign. Wristrest is an Addit product marketed in Australia and New Zealand. Designed to fit under a computer keyboard, Wristrest helps prevent repetitive strain injury, a term encompassing a range of medical problems caused by repetitive action

アディットは、コンピュータの付加製品を製造販売する。その名は〈add it＝それを付け加えるという〉会社の役割を示すよう選ばれている。歯切れがよく覚えやすい社名は、抽象的なプラスの記号を使ったシンボルマークによって強調されている。コンピュータのキーボードの下につけて手首をのせるリストレストは、手の緊張の繰り返しによる障害を防ぐためのものである。

HYATT SAUJANA

The Hyatt Saujana is a first class hotel located a few minutes from Kuala Lumpur airport. Adjacent to a lush, international standard golf course, the hotel attracts a large clientele of business people. Each Hyatt hotel conforms to particular guidelines yet each retains its own individual identity. The area surrounding the Hyatt Saujana features numerous palm trees and this provided the inspiration for the visual identity program we developed

ハイアット・サウジャナは、クアラルンプル空港から車で数分のところにある第一級のホテル。緑したたる国際級ゴルフコースに隣接し、ハイアット系列のホテルは、その独自性も備えている。それぞれの独自性も備えている。そのガイドラインを守っているが、ハイアット系列のホテルは、ビジネスマンの宿泊客が多い。まわりに生えた無数の椰子が、われわれの開発したヴィジュアルアイデンティティプログラムに、インスピレーションを与えてくれた。

FISHERMAN'S CORNER

JAPANESE SHRIMPS
Juicy shrimps rolled in rice vermicelli and deep-fried.
Tempura sauce on the side
$ 13.50

FILLET OF IKAN KURAU
Pan-fried and accompanied by lemon butter and almonds
$ 8.50

$ 6.50
$ 3.50

$ 3.50

$ 5.90

$ 3.50

$ 6.90

7.90

.40

room service menu

bayu lounge

BECTON CORPORATION PTY LTD

Becton Corporation is a major property developer responsible for a number of innovative building projects. Our task was to develop a visual identity program for the company and to design a corporate book with the aim of communicating their activities to financiers, institutions and corporations who are all likely tenants of the buildings they construct. In one publication, Becton Corporation was able to establish its strength, focus its philosophy, demonstrate the quality of its developments and calibre of its tenants and finally, communicate the support it receives from the financial community. The launch of the book (pictured) was timed to coincide with the opening of the company's new premises, a building clad in black marble

ベクトン・コーポレイションは、大手の建築開発会社で数多くの革新的なビル建設プロジェクトを行なってきた。われわれは、ヴィジュアルアイデンティティプログラムの開発と、投資家や、ビルのテナントになりそうな企業や組織に対し、ベクトン・コーポレイションの活動を伝えるパンフレットをデザインした。このパンフレットの刊行により、ベクトン・コーポレイションは、その力量を大いに示し、経営理念を明確にし、開発事業の質の高さやビルのテナントの性格を明らかにし、金融界から得ている信頼をクライアントに伝えることができたのである。なお、パンフレットの刊行は、黒大理石の新しいベクトン・コーポレイションビルのオープニングにあわせて行なわれた。

'...ranked amongst the top commercial development companies...'

'...an enviable reputation for completing projects on time and to budget...'

BECTON CORPORATION PTY LTD

Becton Corporation also produces information booklets about each of the projects it initiates. The spreads shown are from a book designed to promote a city office complex, the Olderfleet Tower. The Olderfleet project involves the integration of a modern office tower with a restored building classified by the National Trust. Our logotype design reflects the gothic architecture of the old building. As is often the case with long term developments such as the Olderfleet Tower, the book was produced prior to the building's construction.

ベクトン・コーポレイションは、一つ一つのプロジェクトのパンフレットも作っている。写真は、都市中心部のオフィス・コンプレックス、オールダー・フリートタワーをプロモートするためにデザインしたもの。オールダー・フリートタワー・プロジェクトは、近代的なオフィスタワーとナショナル・トラスト（文化財保護機関）で修復保護の指定を受けたビルの二つを統合する計画である。われわれの作ったロゴは、その古いビルの方のゴシック建築をもとにしている。長期開発ではよくあるように、オールダー・フリートタワー・プロジェクトのパンフレットも、建設に先立って刊行された。

BROKEN HILL PROPRIETARY CO LTD

The iron and steel producer, BHP, has for many years been Australia's largest company. The BHP Journal is a magazine published regularly by the company's public affairs department. Each issue contains up to 80 pages and includes articles on topics related to the company's activities. The covers and double page spreads pictured here show a diverse range of BHP's interests, designed with a dynamism reflecting the company's personality

鉄・鉄鋼メーカー、BHPは、オーストラリア最大の企業としての長い歴史を誇っている。「BHPジャーナル」は、BHPの広報部が定期的に発行している雑誌で、毎号八〇頁でBHPの活動関連記事を掲載している。ここにあげたのは、表紙と見開き二頁。BHPの活動の多様さが、BHPの方向性を反映するかのようにダイナミックなデザインで表現されている。

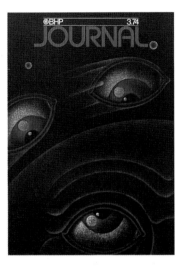

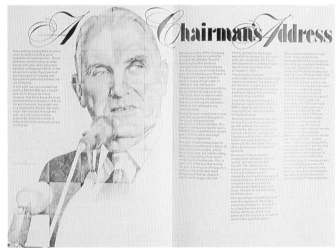

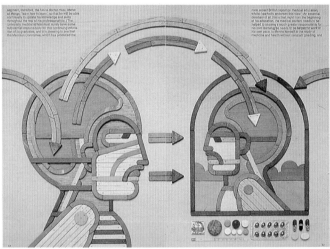

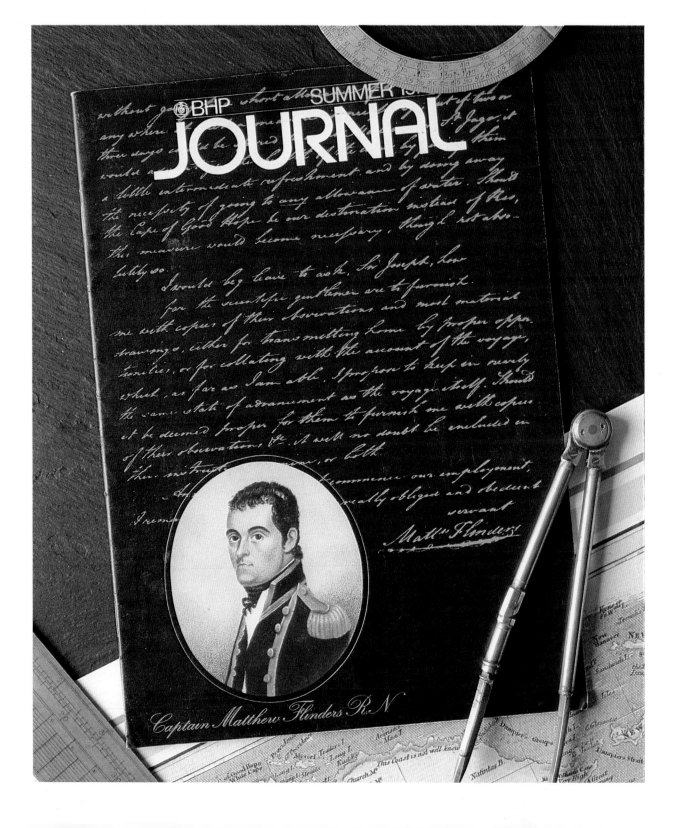

BHP JOURNAL SUMMER

Captain Matthew Flinders R.N.

MOBIL OIL AUSTRALIA LTD

Mobil Oil, one of Australia's major oil companies, reports annually to its employees as well as its shareholders. These are two of the books we have designed and produced for Mobil. The covers and double page spreads of books such as these present a creative challenge in that they must convey the desired corporate image of the company in a simple and imaginative way

146

挑戦といっていいだろう。いる。クリエイティブなコーポレイトイメージをコーポレイトイメージをコーポレイトイメージを伝えることを旨としてゆたかなデザインをシンプルで想像力報告書の表紙と見開きは、われわれが製作した年次報告を出す。それぞれ株主に対し、モービルは職員および大手石油会社、オーストラリアの

Resale continued to break new ground

New approaches developed to meet changing market demands

We asked your opinions

Communication and training prepare employees for changing role

G J COLES & COY LIMITED

G J Coles is the biggest retailer, and almost the biggest company, in Australia.
Established in 1914, the company has progressed steadily until it now operates hundreds
of supermarkets, variety stores, K mart and liquor stores throughout Australia. Coles
employs more than 60,000 people, many of whom are shareholders in the company.
The design of the Report to Shareholders pictured here reflects the length and breadth
of the company's operation in a refreshing and demonstrative way

示している。
斬新な方法ではっきりと
巾広い経営方針を、
デザインは、G・J・コウルズの
ここにみられる株主への報告書の
六万人を越し、多くは株主である。
運営するほどになった。職員は
マーケット、Kマート酒屋を
全国に数百におよぶスーパー
着実に発展を続け、オーストラリア
企業である。一九一四年の創立以来、
すべての企業の中でもおそらく最大の
小売業界の最大手で、オーストラリアの
G・J・コウルズはオーストラリア

THE AUSTRALIAN BALLET FOUNDATION

This is the cover and a double page spread from one of many Australian Ballet Foundation Annual Reports we have designed. Although the content of annual reports is essentially financial, the graphic solutions in this case emanate from a greater creative latitude than is usual

われわれが
デザインした
多数の
オーストラリアン・
バレエ財団年次
報告書の中から、
表紙と見開き
二頁。年次報告の
内容の本質は
財政報告だが、
ここでは
グラフィックを
使って創造性を
強調した。

Tricontinental is an innovative merchant banking organisation with a philosophy of supporting entrepreneurial ideas and growing with them. In the company's annual report "A review of 1986 and the future", we developed a theme to reflect this preparedness to invest in inspiration. Shown are the front covers of the two main sections within the report and an interior double page spread

150

トライコンティネンタルは、
企業家精神旺盛なアイディアを
後援し、それとともに成長する
という企業理念を持った
革新的な商業銀行グループ
である。その年次報告書
「一九八六年の概観と予測」
の中でわれわれは、
ひらめきで投資するという
彼等の意欲を反映する
テーマを追求した。
ここにのせたのは、その
報告書の主要部分二箇所と
見開きである。

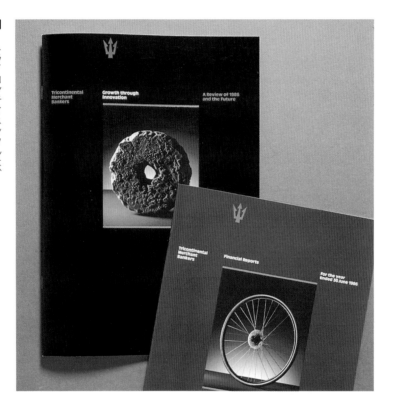

PROJECT FINANCE

STATE BANK OF VICTORIA

When one of Australia's major banking institutions, the State Bank of Victoria, constructed an imposing office tower as its headquarters, much of the building was available for leasing to other companies. We designed and produced this book to serve as an information document for the leasing agents to give to prospective tenants. The book presents the features of the State Bank Centre, including its location, architecture, office environment, views and security system. Also, its sophisticated lift service was represented graphically as shown on these pages

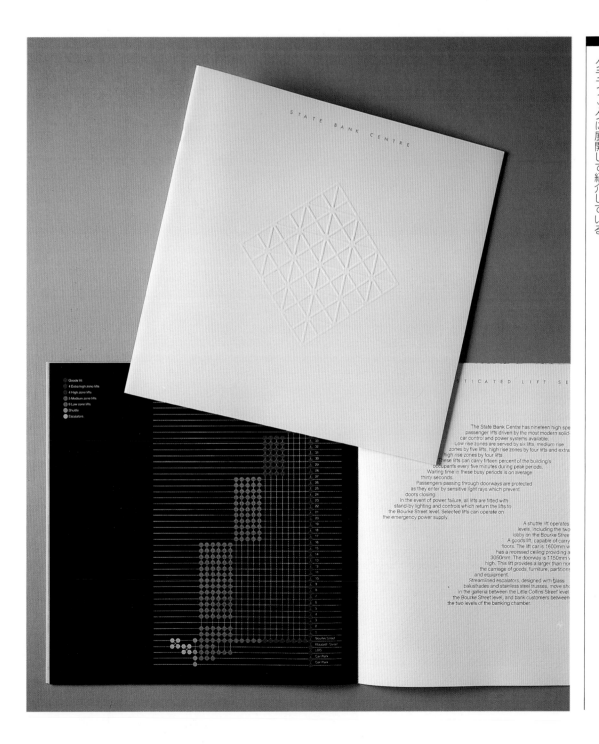

オーストラリアの大手都市銀行、ヴィクトリア州立銀行は、本店社屋としてヴィクトリア州立銀行センターという高層ビルを建築した。建物内部の多くは、他の企業へのリーススペースになっている。われわれは不動産業者が、入居予定のテナントに建物の情報を提供できるように、この小冊子をデザイン・刊行した。ヴィクトリア州立銀行センタービルの地域性、建築の状況、ビジネス環境、眺望、安全警備システムなどの特長を盛りこんだものである。またここにかかげたように、洗練されたエレベーターシステムも、グラフィックに展開して紹介している。

The State Bank Centre has nineteen high spe[...] passenger lifts driven by the most modern solid-[...] car control and power systems available. Low rise zones are served by six lifts, medium rise zones by five lifts, high rise zones by four lifts and extra[...] high rise zones by four lifts. [...]ese lifts can carry fifteen percent of the building's occupants every five minutes during peak periods. Waiting time in these busy periods is on average thirty seconds. Passengers passing through doorways are protected as they enter by sensitive light rays which prevent doors closing. In the event of power failure, all lifts are fitted with stand-by lighting and controls which return the lifts to the Bourke Street level. Selected lifts can operate on the emergency power supply.

A shuttle lift operates [...] levels, including the two [...] lobby on the Bourke Stree[...] A goods lift, capable of carry[...] floors. The lift car is 1600mm w[...] has a recessed ceiling providing a [...] 3050mm. The doorway is 1150mm v[...] high. This lift provides a larger than nor[...] the carriage of goods, furniture, partitions and equipment. Streamlined escalators, designed with glass balustrades and stainless steel trusses, move sho[...] in the galleria between the Little Collins Street[...] the Bourke Street level, and bank customers between the two levels of the banking chamber.

CADBURY SCHWEPPES PTY LTD

Tarax is a popular brand of soft drinks and flavoured mineral waters. We were commissioned to design a new image for their range of soft drinks in bottles and cans. The symbol we developed features refreshing colours and a vivacious character which we then adapted to the label designs. In subsequent advertisements, posters and window signs, the symbol became a strong graphic element that was easily recognised. Since then, the company has produced a range of mineral waters, also in bottles and cans. When we devised the packaging for this range, we emphasised the natural fruit flavours and presented the products simply and with great appeal

「タラックス」は、ソフトドリンクとフレイバーをつけたミネラルウォーターの人気ブランドである。カドベリー・シュウェップスは、ビン、カン、いずれにも新しいイメージが欲しいといってきた。そこでわれわれはシンボルマークに、気分を壮快にするような色を使って、陽気で活発な感じのキャラクターを作り出し、これをラベルのデザインにも展開した。それに付随したコマーシャルやポスター、あるいは店頭に貼るステッカーなどで、このシンボルマークはそれぞれのデザインの中で非常に強力な、目をひくグラフィック性を持つようになった。その後カドベリー・シュウェップスは新たなミネラルウォーターのシリーズをこれもビンとカンで発表したが、われわれは果物の自然なフレイバーを強調し、シンプルながら強いアピールをもつ商品をデザインした。

LINDEMANS WINES PTY LTD

Lindemans Wines range from what is undoubtedly the most popular table wine in Australia to some of the most highly regarded. More than sixty bottled wines carry the Lindemans label. With such a range, it comes as no surprise to learn that the company can trace its history back to 1843. More recently, the wine market has diversified into such products as cask wines and wine based drinks. Apart from the numerous labels we have designed for Lindemans bottled wines, we have also developed identities for the broad variety of cask and wine-based products the company now markets, including Tropicana Cooler, Castaway Cooler and Liebestein

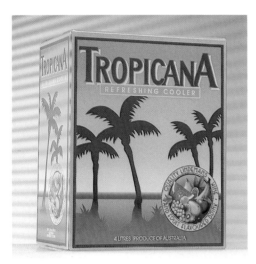

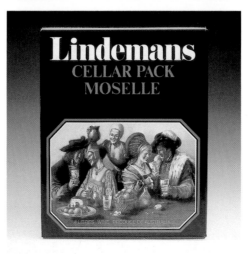

リンデマンズ・ワインズは、オーストラリアで
最もポピュラーなテーブルワインから、
最高級ワインに至るまでを扱い、リンデマンズの
ラベルをつけるワインの種類は六〇を超える。
この多様性を考えれば、リンデマンズの社史が
一八四三年にさかのぼるときかされても不思議は
ないだろう。最近ワイン市場は、カスクワイン
（箱詰め）からワインをベースにした飲み物に
至るまで多種に多様化しており、われわれは多種に
わたるワインのビンのラベルデザインの他に、
カスクワインや、「トロピカーナ・クーラー」
「カースタウェイ・クーラー」「リーベスティン」
などワインをベースにした飲み物の
アイデンティティを作った。

Mediscience is a company based in Singapore which exports a number of food brands. We developed the identities for Eliya and Madras canned and pre-cooked curried meals. These products are sold not only in Singapore but in Malaysia, Canada and Europe as well

メディサイエンスは、シンガポールに本拠を置く食品メーカー。多数のブランドを輸出しているが、われわれはカレーのカン詰め「エリヤ」と「マドラス」のアイデンティティを開発した。この二つのブランドはシンガポールはもとより、マレーシア、カナダ、そしてヨーロッパの市場に出されている。

MALAYAN BREWERIES (S) PTE LTD

Lion Stout is brewed and sold locally by Malayan Breweries. The drink has a mystique in Malaysia that is associated with its legendary medicinal qualities. It is well liked for its warm, rich, healthy image. The label design we developed depicts a visual representation of the product's name not only to strengthen its branding but also to symbolise strength

「ライオンスタウト」はマレイアン・ブルーワリーズが醸造し、国内販売している。このビールは、マレーシアでは薬効があるという伝統と結びついて、一種神秘的な雰囲気を持ち、暖かみ、コク、健康というイメージで広く知られている。われわれが作ったラベルは、「ライオンスタウト」という名前を視覚化し、「ライオン…」という名前の強さだけでなく、製品の強さも象徴している。

Kayser is a well known brand of hosiery marketed by Australian Consolidated Hosiery. When the company released a new range of coloured pantyhose, we were asked to develop the packaging. As there are 101 colours offered in the range, our solution was to employ simple graphics in black and white over a celluloid pack to allow the colours to speak for themselves

158

「カイザー」はオーストラリアン・コンソリデイテッド・ホージャリーのパンティストッキング。カラーシリーズを発表するシリーズを発表する際にわれわれにパッケージデザインを依頼してきた。このシリーズには一〇一色のバリエーションがあるため製品の色を生かしてパッケージ全体をセロファンの包装でおおい、その上に黒と白でシンプルなグラフィックをのせた。

オーストラリアン・フェザー・ミルズは「アーティックダウン」というダウンと羽根のコンチネンタルキルトと、枕のシリーズを製造販売している。そのアイデンティティを作るためわれわれは明確なロゴをデザインし、パッケージにつけた。またダウンと羽根の割合に応じてロゴの色をいくつかに使い分けている。

ARTICDOWN

MADE IN · AUSTRALIA

AUSTRALIA'S OWN ALL SEASON
CONTINENTAL QUILT

CONTAINS 50% PURE DOWN 50% FEATHER
DESIGNED WITH FEATURES THAT WILL HELP
YOU SLEEP COMFORTABLY FOR MANY YEARS.
SPECIFICALLY MADE FOR AUSTRALIA'S UNIQUE
CONDITIONS WITH ONLY FIRST GRADE
MATERIALS FOR COMFORT AND DURABILITY.

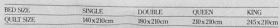

BED SIZE	SINGLE	DOUBLE	QUEEN	KING
QUILT SIZE	140 x 210cm	180 x 210cm	210 x 210cm	245 x 210cm

SELECTION GUIDE   For the ultimate in comfort, extra warmth and lightness choose a high down content quilt. For security of weight, medium warmth and comfort choose a high-feather content quilt.

FELTEX (NZ) LIMITED

Feltex manufacture and market internationally the Slumberwool range of pure woollen underlay blankets. A sheep was included in the design on the front of the pack to clearly identify the origin and purpose of the product. The back of the pack was designed to look rather like an advertisement promoting the beneficial features of sleeping on a blanket of wool. The Slumberwool mark was used on the company's stationery items, including business cards and letterheads

PREMIER MILK

In Singapore and Malaysia, Daisy brand milk is well known. Diet Daisy low fat milk is one of the firmly established range of Daisy products. Our task was to develop a packaging design with a contemporary and healthy appearance to reflect the nature of the product

フェルテックスは、純毛の下敷用毛布、「スランバーウール」シリーズを製造し、海外にも輸出している。パックの表のデザインには、羊を一頭あしらい、製品の品質表示とその価値を明確にしている。「スランバーウール」のシンボルマークは、フェルテックス社の名刺、便せんなどの事務用品にも使われている。

「デイジー」ブランドのミルクは、シンガポールやマレーシアでよく知られている。乳脂肪分を低くおさえた「ダイエットデイジーミルク」は、デイジーシリーズでも安定した市場を持つ製品。われわれはこの製品の性格を反映する、現代的で健康な外観のパッケージをデザインした。

ARTEMUS

Artemus sells interesting and exclusive fashions for young women. The visual identity we developed for the company reflects a soft feminine quality which is in keeping with the style of the clothes marketed through the stores

アーティマスは
若い女性
向けの独自な
スタイルを持つ
高級ファッション
メーカー。
われわれの
開発した
ヴィジュアル
アイデンティティは、
そのスタイルと
マッチした
やわらかな女性らしさを
表現
している。

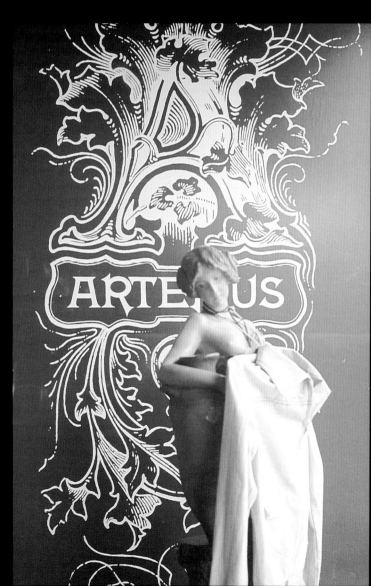

TROLLOPE SILVERWOOD + BECK

Silverwood & Beck was one of Australia's oldest manufacturing shopfitting companies. When it became part of Trollope Displays, the resulting company needed an expanded identity to include its new dimension of production. TS&B were now 'designers and manufacturers of corporate identity retail merchandising commercial interiors', a wordy description of their role yet it was possible to incorporate this function into the symbol pictured. The logo embodies an honest representation of the company's personality and philosophy. The 'T' for Trollope has been emphasised to clearly show its dominant role in the company's operation

シルバーウッド・アンド・ベックは、オーストラリア有数の歴史を誇る商店備品メーカーだった。トロロープ・ディスプレイ社がこれを吸収したため新しく成立した企業は、より巾の広いアイデンティティが必要となってきた。TS&Bは現在、新合併によって加わった商品ラインを含んだ、"CIも含んだトータルなインテリアのデザイナーでありメーカー"となっている。このことばによる表現を視覚的なシンボルにしたわけである。ロゴはTS&Bの性格とフィロソフィーを素直に表現したもので、TS&Bの中でトロロープが主要な役割を果たしていることを明確にするためにトロロープの「T」は、強調されている。

Epicurean is the official journal of the Wine and Food Society of Australia. Published six times a year, the magazine contains articles of interest to lovers of fine foods and wines. Prior to a change of publishers, we had a long association with the magazine and designed and produced many complete issues. Our cover designs and illustrations position the magazine as interesting, unusual and eminently readable. This identity is certainly supported by the contents of each issue

164

毎回ちがっている。
カバーのイメージは各号の内容によって
読みやすいとの評価を得ている。
はおもしろく、ユニークできわめて
レーションにより「エピキュリアン」
われわれのカバーデザインとイラスト
製作まですべてをまかされている。
つきあいがあり、デザインから
以前から、われわれはこの雑誌と
出版元が現在の会社に変わるずっと
そのある記事をのせ、年六回発行。
美食家、ワイン愛飲家の関心を
ワイン・フード協会の機関誌。
「エピキュリアン」はオーストラリア・

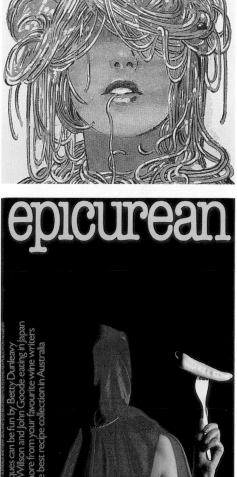

Cooper Veterinary Products is a subsidiary of Wellcome New Zealand. The company markets the Panacur range of veterinary and pharmaceutical products to service the country's biggest industry, the raising of sheep for wool and meat. Initially we designed the packaging for Panacur products and then, as part of a promotional campaign, we designed and produced a series of complementary calendar posters. Each one featured a compelling illustration of a different breed of sheep and contained information about Panacur products and offered veterinary advice to graziers. The posters appeared as inserts in rural magazines

クーパー・ヴェテリナリー・プロダクツは
ウェルカム・ニュージーランドの子会社で、
畜産用医薬品、「パナカー」シリーズを
出し、ニュージーランド最大の産業である
羊毛および羊肉生産に貢献している。
まずわれわれは、「パナカー」シリーズの
パッケージデザインを行ない、後に
販売促進キャンペーンの一環として、
ポスターカレンダーをデザイン製作した。
これは一枚々々にちがう品種の羊を
人目をひくイラストで描いて、パナカー製品に
ついての説明文を付記し、対象となる
牧羊農家に対して、畜産学的助言をそえたもので、
農業雑誌数誌にとじ込まれた。

NOVEMBER		1982	DECEMBER		1982		JANUARY		1983
S		14 28	S		12 26		S		9 23
	1	15 29			13 27				10 24
	2	16 30			14 28				11 25
	3	17		1	15 29				12 26
	4	18		2	16 30				13 27
	5	19		3	17 31				14 28
	6	20		4	18			1	15 29
S	7	21	S	5	19		S	2	16 30
	8	22		6	20			3	17 31
	9	23		7	21			4	18
	10	24		8	22			5	19
	11	25		9	23			6	20
	12	26		10	24			7	21
	13	27		11	25			8	22

N.Z. SHEEP CALENDAR
—1982-83—
PANACUR
FOR TARGET LIVEWEIGHTS
MANAGEMENT TIPS

Hogget growth is at its peak potential (up to 140g (½lb) day). Careful management of feed is needed to make the best of the situation. Optimum pasture levels should be equivalent to 1200-1400 RDM4/ha where possible. About 5-6cm (2-2¼ins) of dense pasture. Even low levels of worm infestation can reduce growth rates. A drench during December for hoggets is a worthwhile precaution considering the November, December rise in available infective larvae. Pasture above the 3cm (1¼in) level after drenching means less infective larvae are available to stock. Keep pasture below seed head where possible to maximise growth.

COOPER

FEBRUARY 1983

S	6	20
	7	21
	8	22
	9	23
	10	24
	11	25
	12	26
S	13	27
	14	28
	1	15
	2	16
	3	17
	4	18
	5	19

MARCH 1983

S	6	20
	7	21
	8	22
	9	23
	10	24
	11	25
	12	26
S	13	27
	14	28
	1	15	29
	2	16	30
	3	17	31
	4	18
	5	19

APRIL 1983

S	3	17
	4	18
	5	19
	6	20
	7	21
	8	22
	9	23
S	10	24
	11	25
	12	26
	13	27
	14	28
	1	15	29
	2	16	30

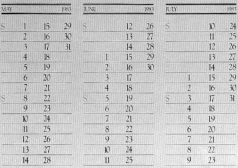

MAY 1983

S	1	15	29
	2	16	30
	3	17	31
	4	18
	5	19
	6	20
	7	21
S	8	22
	9	23
	10	24
	11	25
	12	26
	13	27
	14	28

JUNE 1983

S	12	26
	13	27
	14	28
	1	15	29
	2	16	30
	3	17
	4	18
S	5	19
	6	20
	7	21
	8	22
	9	23
	10	24
	11	25

JULY 1983

S		10	24
		11	25
		12	26
		13	27
		14	28
	1	15	29
	2	16	30
S	3	17	31
	4	18
	5	19
	6	20
	7	21
	8	22
	9	23

YOUNG PRESIDENTS ORGANISATION

The Young Presidents Organisation is an international association formed for people who have achieved a high level of business success at an early age. The organisation arranges conferences around the world encouraging high achievers to maintain and improve their business status. Pictured is the visual identity program we developed for the 1988 Young Presidents Organisation conference to be held in Sydney, Australia. The theme for this conference is 'The best of Australia'

オブ・オーストラリア」である。
今回の会議のテーマは「ザ・ベスト・
アイデンティティプログラムである。
ために開発した、ヴィジュアル
シドニーで開かれる会議の
一九八八年にオーストラリアの
ここでとりあげたのは、
世界中で会議を開く。
地位を維持、向上させるため、
青年実業家のビジネス上の
人々の国際組織。そうした
若くしてビジネスに成功した
オーガナイゼイションは、
ヤング・プレジデンツ・

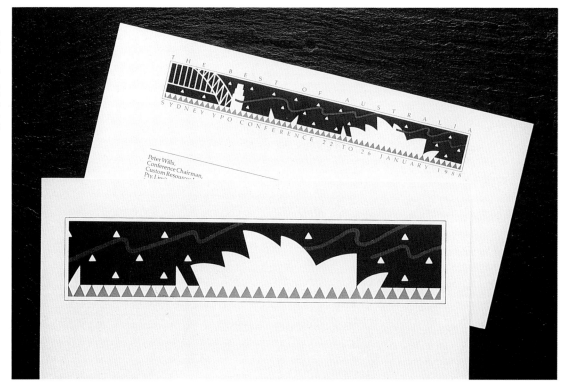

OXFORD UNIVERSITY PRESS AUSTRALIA

We were asked to update the identity of Oxford University Press and the symbol
we developed, based on the letter 'O', incorporates the company's literary personality.
Recently the company released a range of new edition dictionaries. We designed the
covers for each of the five versions, ranging in size from pocket book to large, heavy
volumes. We used a series of literary marks in the word 'Oxford' to reflect the purpose
of the books

以前われわれは、オックスフォード・
ユニバーシティ・プレスのために、
「O」の文字を基本に、出版社の
文学的な性格を反映したシンボルマークを
作った。今回、オックスフォード・
ユニバーシティ・プレスのアイデンティティを
更に今日的なものにするよう
依頼された。それが最近刊行された
五種類の辞書（新版）の表紙デザインである。
辞書のサイズは、ポケット版から
大きく厚い巻にわたった。
辞書の機能を反映させるため、
OXFORDということばに、五つの
辞書に共通な記号をあしらった。

ARTS VICTORIA

Arts Victoria is a program of triennial arts festivals held throughout the State of Victoria in Australia. Each festival is based on a different aspect of the arts. We designed a symbol for Arts Victoria which is based on the stylised letters 'A' and 'V' to suggest waving banners, a traditionally festive image. The symbol design remains constant, with the colours changing for each festival. The design project included development of the symbol, stationery, brochures and posters

A state wide festival of the visual arts

Arts Victoria 75

exhibitions and activities in

Melbourne
Ararat
Ballarat
Benalla
Bendigo
Castlemaine
Geelong
Hamilton
Horsham

Langwarrin
Mildura
Mornington
Morwell
Sale
Shepparton
Swan Hill
Warrnambool

24 March
15 November
1975

THE ADELAIDE FESTIVAL

The Adelaide Festival is recognised throughout the world as one of Australia's most significant arts events. The material shown here formed the basis of a visual identity program for the Adelaide Festival. We devised a simple graphic system for the vast amount of material produced to promote the Festival's events. As a unifying element, we designed a multi faceted symbol which could be used in whole or in part. The symbol combines three images relevant to the Festival. First, a stylised letter 'A' symbolising Adelaide and the Arts. Second, a stylised human form symbolising performers and spectators. Third, a stylised eye symbolising the visual nature of the Festival. The brochures and information folder shown here demonstrate the powerful versatility of the graphic treatment

アーツ・ヴィクトリアは、オーストラリアのヴィクトリア州全域で行なわれるさまざまな分野のトリエンナーレ芸術祭である。われわれが作ったシンボルマークは、伝統的に祭りのイメージを持つのぼりがひるがえっているところを暗示しており、様式化された「A」と「V」を基本とする。それぞれの芸術祭はこのシンボルマークのデザインを色を変えて使っている。デザインプロジェクトは、シンボルマークの開発の他、事務用品、パンフレット、ポスターの製作まで広範囲に及んだ。

アデレイド芸術祭は、オーストラリアで最も重要な芸術祭の一つとして、国際的に評価されている。ここにのせたのは、そのヴィジュアルアイデンティティプログラムの基本となったもの。芸術祭のイベントをプロモートする膨大な量の宣伝物のためにシンプルなグラフィックシステムを作った。それを統合する要素は、全体としても部分としても使える多面性を持つシンボルマークである。これは芸術祭にふさわしい三つのイメージを組み合わせたもので、まず、アデレードとアーツを象徴する「A」。次は演者と観客を象徴する人体。そして芸術祭の視覚性を象徴する目である。ここにのせたパンフレットとそれを入れるホールダーに、グラフィックの強力な自在性をごらんいただけるはずである。

JEANS EXPRESS

When the well established jeans marketer, Cheap Jeans, was repositioned and renamed as Jeans Express, we were asked to develop a new visual identity program to accommodate the transition. The program was implemented in the stages shown here and the logotype and mark for Jeans Express were eventually used on shop signage, packaging, the products themselves and on stationery

安定した市場を持つジーンズ販売会社、チープジーンズは、機構改革を行ない、社名を改めた。その際われわれは、この変化を表現する新しいヴィジュアルアイデンティティプログラムの開発を依頼された。プログラムはここに示したような段階を経て行なわれ、ロゴとシンボルマークは最終的に店の看板、パッケージ、製品、事務用品に使用された。

Stage 1   Stage 2   Stage 3

CLUNIES-ROSS AUSTRALIA PTY LTD

Clunies-Ross Australia manufacture and market a range of high quality fabrics
and papers under the brand name 'Australiana'. The range is marketed both locally
and internationally and has achieved particular success in the United States. The fabric
and paper designs are based on Aboriginal motifs and traditional Australian landscape
colours and textures. As part of the visual identity program, we designed a stylised 'A'
using three patterns and a variety of colours reflecting the style of the range of products.
The logotype was used on stationery items, labels and pattern books

クルニーズ・ロス・オーストラリアは、
「オーストラリアーナ」という
ブランド名で高品質の織物と紙を製造、
オーストラリア内外で販売し、特に
アメリカで好評を博している。製品の
デザインは、オーストラリア原住民の
モチーフ、および昔ながらのオーストラリアの
風景の色彩と質感を基本とする。
ヴィジュアルアイデンティティプログラムの
一部として、三つのパターンを、
また製品のスタイルを反映する一群の
色を使って、「A」の文字をデザインした。
このロゴは事務用品、ラベル、
パターン見本帖に使われ
ている。

AUSTRALIANA

To promote the international World Expo 88, an identity was developed to project a sense of festivity, dynamism, vitality and enjoyment. The function of the central symbol was to suggest many of the varied experiences and events being staged during Expo 88. The six abstract 'sails' depict the key Expo attractions which include an amusement park, cultural exhibition, fireworks and laser shows, pop and classical orchestras, and colourful parades. The environmental graphics shown were used on a range of outdoor sites.

われわれはワールド・エクスポ・八八の
プロモーションのため、お祭りの
雰囲気、ダイナミズム、それに楽しさを
盛り上げるアイデンティティを
開発した。シンボルマークの役割は、
会期中のさまざまなイベントに対する
期待を持たせることである。
六つの「帆」は、遊園地、いろいろな
文化的展示、花火、レーザーショー、
ポップおよびクラシックコンサート、
それにカラフルなパレードという六つの
アトラクションを表している。
ここにとりあげた環境グラフィックは、
屋外でさまざまに使用されている。

DELVA INTERNATIONAL

Delva International manufacture and market a vast range of hair care products. Shape Up is a light perming solution used by men as well as women, a consideration which influenced the final packaging design. To create a modern, stylish personality for the product, a simple, elegant logotype was developed to reflect the properties of the product. This was reinforced by the 'kiss curl' symbol also featured in different colours to enable identification of the varying strengths of the perming solution

デルヴァ・インターナショナルは、ヘアケア製品を幅広く製造し、販売する。「シェイプアップ」シリーズは男女共用のパーマ液。その男女共用のパーマ液をポイントにパッケージデザインをした。ロゴは、モダンでスタイリッシュな性格を表現するよう、簡潔でエレガントなものにした。「キス・カール」のシンボルマークもこれに呼応する。ロゴとシンボルマークはパーマ液の濃度に応じ、さまざまな色が使用されている。

「ケン」はリシス社の香水。シンガポールのリシスは、本来金の蘭のペンダントなど土産物メーカーである。この高級香水とオーデコロンは、真夜中にだけ咲き、質素にして甘やかな香りを放つという花から名づけられた。「ケン・ファ」という花からその花をかたどり、ボトルはその花をかたどり、パッケージの色は香りがもっとも豊かな真夜中を暗示している。

RISIS PTE LTD

Kheng is a perfume manufactured by Risis, a Singapore company which traditionally produces gold-plated orchid pendants and other souvenirs for tourists. This exclusive perfume in concentrate and cologne is named after the Keng Hwa, a shy flower that blooms only at midnight and releases a fresh and enjoyable, simple yet sweet fragrance. The bottles are based on the shape of the flower and the colour of the outer packaging suggests midnight when the fragrance is at its most potent

BRYANT & MAY PTY LTD

For many years, Bryant & May have manufactured the most famous brand of matches
in Australia. They have a sound tradition in the lights market with this and other match
products. More recently, there have been dramatic changes in the use of matches and,
in particular, the habits of smokers. Disposable lighters are the most common method
of lighting cigarettes. Bryant & May developed Citylights, the product shown, and we
developed the packaging and counter display to more closely reflect the demands
of contemporary city life

ブライアント・アンド・メイは
長年にわたり、オーストラリアで
最も有名なブランドのマッチを
作って業界でも確固とした地位と
伝統を誇ってきた。最近ではマッチの
使用に、とりわけ喫煙の習慣に
大きな変化が起こり、現在では
使い捨てライターが主流である。
ブライアント・アンド・メイも
ここにのせた「シティライト」という
ライターを開発した。そこで
われわれは、今日のシティライフが
要請するものを、さらによく反映する
パッケージとカウンターディスプレイをデザインした。

24 DISPOSABLE LIGHTERS FROM BRYANT & MAY

THE CASCADE BREWERY COMPANY

The Cascade Brewery Company has been brewing beer since 1824 in Tasmania, the only island state of Australia. Recently the company introduced a new product to compete in the imported and premium beer segment of the market. To maximise the visibility of Cascade Premium Lager, the labels feature the famous Tasmanian Tiger, an extinct animal once found only in Tasmania. Its image also appears on a barrel above the main gates of the brewery

カスケイド・ブルーワリー・カンパニーは、創業一八二四年の古い歴史を誇るタスマニア州のビール醸造会社。最近、「カスケイド・プレミアラガー」を発表、輸入・高級ビール部門にうって出た。ラベルには、アイ・キャッチャーとして、タスマニア島にのみ棲息し、今は絶滅したタスマニア・タイガーをあしらった。このタスマニア・タイガーは本社正門上のビヤ樽にもつけられている。

「ラガー」と「ライトエール」のカンビールは、元のデザインを生かしつつデザインしなおし、創業当時の工場のイラストをあしらった。

CUSTOM RESOURCES INTERNATIONAL PTY LTD

CRI is a property developing company offering a complete service to customers, from the initial planning of a project to the management of its construction. CRI is backed by Custom Credit and this was one of the considerations in developing an identity program. The symbol is flexible enough to carry a number of interpretations related to growth and building. It appears on stationery, signage for hoardings, the company newsletter architectural drawings and the book (pictured) outlining the company's philosophy. In the company's head office, it has been reproduced as a three dimensional sculpture

184

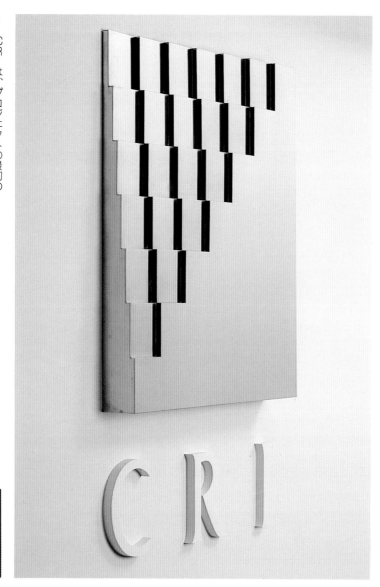

CRIは、プロジェクトの最初の
プランニングから建設のマネージメントに
至るまで、すべてのサービスを提供する
開発会社。カスタム・クレジットの
後援を受けており、その点も
アイデンティティプログラムを作る上で
考慮した。シンボルマークは、成長と
建設に対する様々な解釈を、できるかぎり
柔軟性を持たせてとりいれて
いる。同シンボルは会社の
建設現場の板囲い、社報、建築図面、
CRI社の方針を述べたパンフレット
(写真入り) につけられている他、
本社には彫刻となっておかれて
いる。

An independent property proposal that appeals to your intelligence not just your emotions

You can judge a company
by the company it keeps

Custom Resources International Pty Ltd. is a joint venture between Custom Credit Corporation Limited and the Executive Directors of CRI, Messrs Peter Wills, Peter Barnes and Jonathan Chambers.
Custom Credit, one of Australia's largest financiers, has assets of around $3 billion in addition to shareholders' funds of approximately $300 million and is wholly-owned by the National Australia Bank, whose assets exceed $35 billion.
CRI's backing is substantial by any standards.

Mr Peter Wills, the Company's Managing Director, has had vast experience in property development, technical services and business management. He is regarded by his peers as one of the most talented and respected in his field.
Mr Peter Barnes' background encompasses accounting and management relating specifically to the construction/property industry. He has held a number of positions including that of Chief Executive Officer with direct responsibility for portfolio management, including investment evaluation, acquisition and development.
Mr Jon Chambers has extensive experience in financial analysis in addition to development and economic analysis, having been involved in industrial, commercial and retail development projects.
In essence, the joint venture has brought together a solid financial backing in tandem with the finest of independent professional advice.

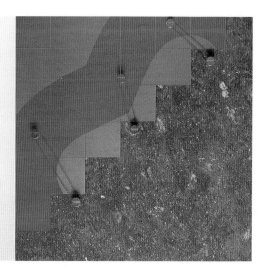

A Moving Development

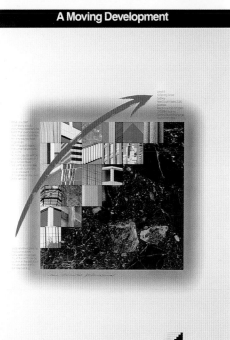

Level 9
10 Spring Street
Sydney
New South Wales 2000
Australia
Telephone (02) 233 2100
Telex (number)
Sydney Stock Exchange

CRI

CRI will back its judgement with firm total commitment.
By undertaking a principal's role in association with the owner, we are prepared to back our judgement financially and to be remunerated through out performance.
Alternatively, CRI's development expertise can be assessed by property owners on a fixed fee basis.

Remuneration: not the charge
of the light brigade

AUSTRALIAN CONSOLIDATED PROPERTIES

Australia Consolidated Properties own and operate a bulk grocery store called
Mr Grocer. Our task was to develop a personality for Mr Grocer and express it through
a totally integrated visual identity program. The vast building has ceilings 10 metres high
and offered the opportunity to satisfy both very contemporary and commercial interior
design considerations. Our approach was based on brightly coloured 'pop art' graphics
which were extended throughout the store on display stands and internal signage.
The Mr Grocer symbol was reproduced on stationery, carry bags and labels

186

オーストラリアン・コンソリデイティッド・プロパティーズの経営する大量買い専門食料雑貨店「ミスター・グロウサー」のために開発したヴィジュアルアイデンティティプログラムで表現されている。店は、天井迄の高さが一〇メートルもある巨大な建物で、現代的かつ商業的にもすぐれたインテリアデザインという要請を満たすだけの空間を備えている。基本は、明るい色彩のポップアートグラフィックで、店全体におよぶ店内サインに至るまで、商品棚から買った商品を入れるシンボルマークは事務用品、ミスター・グロウサーのプラスティックバッグ、それにラベルに使われている。

FREEDOM FURNITURE

The image created by this company is one of freedom in terms of furniture design. Their range of products is casual and contemporary. To reflect this attitude, the double E in the logotype has broken away from the rest of the letters. In turn, this approach to comfortable living is supported by the company mark, an abstract repetition of the Es. Both the logotype and the symbol have been designed for use on store signage, stationery, swing tickets and wrapping materials

フリーダム・ファニチュアは、自由な家具デザインというイメージを作り上げた。この方針を反映させるため、ロゴの綴りの中の二つの「E」を際立たせ、抽象性を持たせて並べ、快適な暮らしに対するアプローチを表現した。ロゴもシンボルマークも店用の看板、事務用品、品質表示札、包装に使えるようデザインしてある。商品は現代的でカジュアルである。

SIMPSON PAPER COMPANY

The California based Simpson Paper Company invited twenty four graphic designers from around the world to interpret the word "Sequences" onto a poster made from one of the many papers marketed by the company. These were then sent as promotional pieces to strengthen the image of Simpson Text and Cover papers, to increase communication with the graphic design community and to improve brand awareness among papers users and specifiers. The poster shown here was designed to demonstrate the sequence of the seasons

カリフォルニアに本拠地をおくシンプソン・ペーパー・カンパニーは、かつて二四人のグラフィックデザイナーを世界中から招待し、同社で販売している多種多様の紙から一点を選ばせて、「シークエンス」(推移)という言葉を翻案したポスターを製作したことがある。その後これらのポスターは、プロモーション用に各地へ送られて、シンプソン社の本文用、表紙用製紙のイメージを上げるのに大いに貢献した。この貢献により、グラフィックデザイン界と製紙業界のコミュニケーションが深まり、消費者がこのブランドに対して持つ意識の向上にもつながった。このページのポスターは季節の「推移」をテーマに製作されたもの。

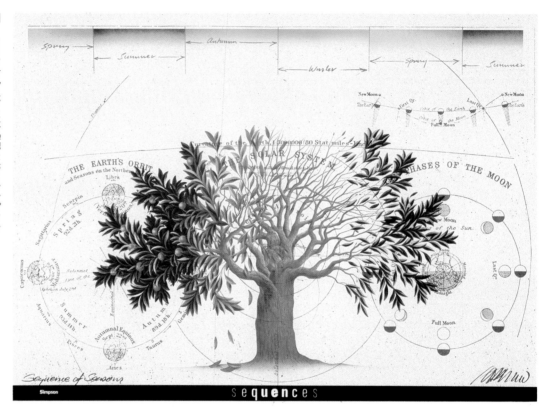

AUSTRALIAN TYPE DIRECTORS CLUB

The Australian Type Directors Club was formed by typographers and art directors to promote excellence in typography and graphic design. We were asked to design the invitation to their third exhibition which was in itself a challenge to set an example

オーストラリアン・
タイプディレクターズ・
クラブは、印刷技術者と
アートディレクターが、
印刷とグラフィック
デザインの質を高める
ことを目的として設立
したもの。われわれは
クラブの第三回展覧会
招待状のデザインを
依頼された。このデザイン
そのものが、高度の印刷
技術の模範となるべく
挑戦した好例となっている。

The visual identity program for the well established printery, Gardner Press, offered
an opportunity to give the name of the company greater meaning than it would have
otherwise. Using symbols related to 'the gardener' and devising an all over pattern for
their letterhead and related stationery items, we were able to graphically show what they
do and how well they do it

190

印刷業界でゆるぎない
地位を誇るガードナー・
プレスのヴィジュアル
アイデンティティプログラムは、
ガードナープレスの名に
さらに深い意味をつけ加えた。
「ガードナー＝庭師」
に関連した様々な
シンボルを使い、
総模様のレターヘッドや
事務用品を工夫することで、
ガードナー・プレスの
企業活動の内容と質を
表現したのである。

GARD NER
CULTIVATING THE CRAFT OF LITHOGRAPHY

GARD NER
CULTIVATING THE CRAFT OF LITHOGRAPHY

WITH COMPLIMENTS

GARDNER PRINTING CO (VIC) PTY LTD 36 THORNTON CRESCENT MITCHAM TELEPHONE (03) 874 2133
ALL CORRESPONDENCE TO BE ADDRESSED TO PO BOX 175 NUNAWADING VICTORIA AUSTRALIA 3131

INTERNATIONAL BARTENDERS ASSOCIATION

Image power cannot always be pinned down to one symbol or one logotype. Sometimes it is apparent in the continuity of presentation of a single idea repeated many times in many different ways. The pictures shown here are taken from a book produced by the International Bartenders Association to commemorate its 25th anniversary. The book was 250 pages long and contained recipes and photographs of more than 300 award winning cocktails created by mixologists from all over the world. So that each recipe could be accompanied by a photograph and detailed description we recreated every cocktail chosen for inclusion. The style of each photograph was determined by the name or colour of the drink and often by its garnishes

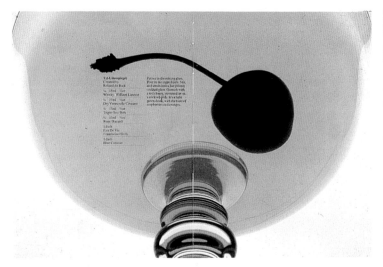

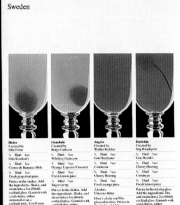

デザイナーが表現しようとするイメージは、常に一つのシンボルマーク、あるいはロゴに集約されるとは限らない。さまざまな折りに、形を変えながらも何度となく繰り返される一つのアイディアのそのつながりの中に、はっきりあらわれてくることもある。

ここにのせたのは、国際バーテンダー連合設立二五周年記念の本からとったもの。この本は全部で二五〇頁を越す、世界中のカクテル名人が一人一人が作り出した三〇〇を越す作り方などくわしい写真および作り方などくわしい説明がつけられている。それぞれの写真のスタイルは、カクテルの名前や色、あるいはそのカクテルのアクセサリーによって決められたものである。

The major computer company, Data General, have a branch in Hong Kong. To send a Chinese New Year greeting to their clients all over the world, we were appointed to develop a calendar based on the Year of the Rabbit

大手コンピュータ会社データ・ジェネラルは香港に支部があり、世界中の顧客に中国暦の年賀状を送るにあたり、われわれに卯年をテーマにしたカレンダーの作成を依頼した。

モナハン・ディマン・アダムズはオーストラリア、ニュージーランド、太平洋沿岸諸国、アメリカに事務所をおく、大きな広告代理店。会計年度半ばに、株主や職員に対し、その間の業績報告書を出し、中間報告を行なっている。すぐれた報告書のデザインは、国際的なコミュニケーショングループとしてのMDAの地位を反映しており、われわれはそれに呼応する簡潔かつ大胆な表紙を製作した。

MONAHAN DAYMAN ADAMS LIMITED

Monahan Dayman Adams is a large advertising agency network with offices throughout Australia, New Zealand, the Pacific and the United States. The half yearly report was designed to communicate to shareholders and staff the company's results for the first six months of the financial year and to mark the halfway point between annual reports. The theme of the report reflects MDA's position as a viable international communications group. This is supported by the design of the simple, bold front cover

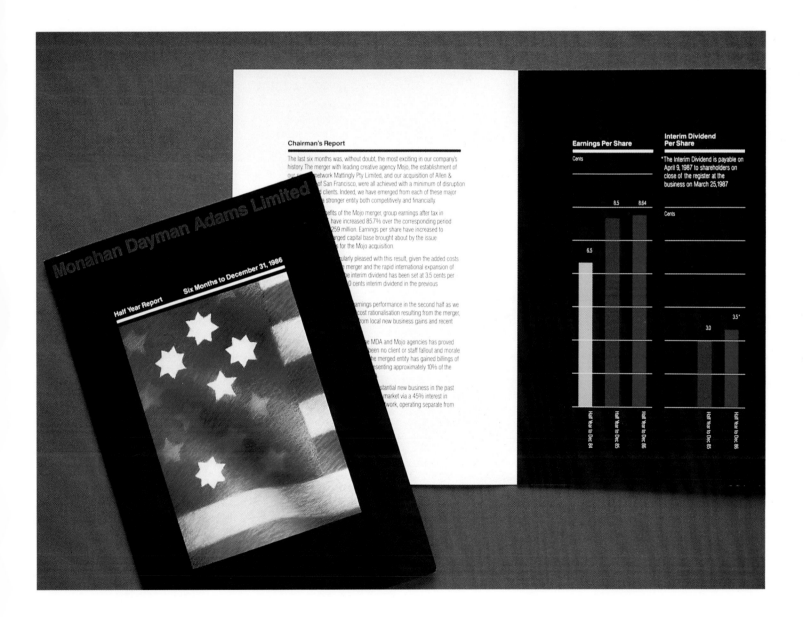

THE SYDNEY
BOULEVARD

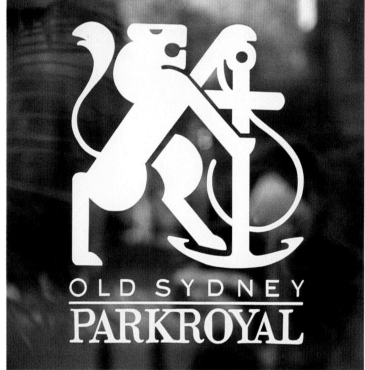

OLD SYDNEY
PARKROYAL

PARKROYAL
CAIRNS

PARKROYAL
BRISBANE

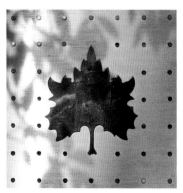

PARKROYAL
ON ST KILDA ROAD

PARKROYAL
ON ST KILDA ROAD

The Southern Pacific Hotel Corporation owns and operates two large hotel chains in Australia, Parkroyal and Travelodge. Recently, both groups were extensively upgraded. We designed a symbol and visual identity program for the parent company, Southern Pacific, and also designed a program to unify all the Parkroyal Hotels. It was important to retain the individual identities of each hotel and, at the same time, introduce a common graphic element to clearly identify the group. Pictured are the identities for each of the Parkroyal Hotels and the mark for the Southern Pacific Hotel Corporation which graphically shows the South Pacific region, the part of the world where the company conducts its business

サザン・パシフィックホテル・コーポレイションは、パーク・ロイヤルおよびトラベロッジという二つの大きなホテルチェーンを所有経営し、最近はこの二つのグループを大巾にグレードアップした。われわれは母胎であるサザン・パシフィックホテル・コーポレイションのシンボルマークと、パーク・ロイヤルホテルを統合するプログラムの他、その際、ヴィジュアルアイデンティティプログラムを作成した。パーク・ロイヤルホテルのアイデンティティを保ちながら、グループ全体の存在をはっきり伝える共通のグラフィックエレメントを生み出す必要があった。ここで紹介したのは、個々のパーク・ロイヤルホテルのアイデンティティとサザン・パシフィックホテル・コーポレイションのシンボルマークである。このシンボルマークは同ホテルのビジネスの舞台となっている南太平洋をグラフィックにしたもの。

Arthur Brunt International Foods market a variety of imported and locally produced food products. The labels shown form part of the total visual identity program we designed for them. Using a symbolic representation of Arthur Brunt himself, the company is able to project its sense of history and integrity in an immediate and appealing way

アーサー・ブラント・インターナショナル・フーズは舶来、国産各種の食品を扱っている。
このラベルは、トータルヴィジュアルアイデンティティプログラムの一部である。
アーサー・ブラントその人の肖像を、象徴的に使い、直接的かつ訴えかけの強い方法で、その歴史と誠実さを投影させることができた。

PROGRESSIVE ENTERPRISES LIMITED

Progressive Enterprises is a large New Zealand company, the owner of three major businesses. Foodtown Supermarkets, 3 Guys Supermarkets and Georgie Pie Restaurants all enjoy a high level of public awareness yet the parent company was largely unknown. We developed a visual identity program designed to promote the company, not only to its employees but to investor groups and the media, too. The symbol we devised suggests progression and growth. Its co ordinated use resulted in an overall cohesion, reinforcing Progressive Enterprises' credibility with its audiences

プログレッシヴ・エンタープライジズは、「フードタウン・スーパーマーケット」「スリーガイズ・スーパーマーケット」それに「ジョージ・パイン・レストランチェーン」の三種類の企業を所有するニュージーランドの大企業。この三つは一つ一つが大きく、それぞれ高い知名度を持つが、母体そのものはほとんど知られていなかった。そこでわれわれは、職員だけでなく、その存在を知らせるためのマスコミに対しても、投資グループやヴィジュアルアイデンティティプログラムを開発した。プログラムの総合的運用により、シンボルマークは進歩と成長をあらためてトータルに確認することができるようになった。

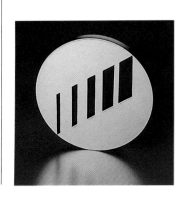

SALLYANNE O'HANLON

Sallyanne O'Hanlon is an Australian interior designer who is well known for the 'modern' art deco style she uses in commercial environments. Her visual identity program reflects this approach to her work with a strong, simple interpretation of her name. The logotype appeared on a range of stationery items and the presentation folder shown.

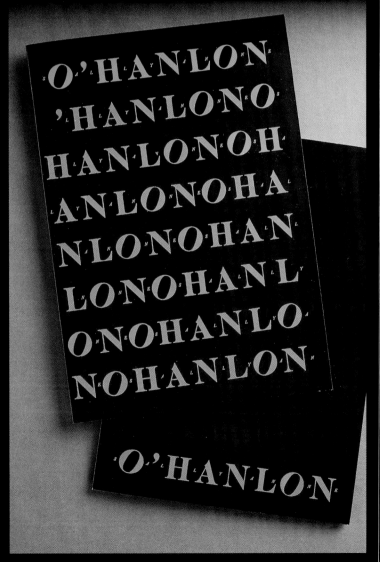

サリー・アン・オハロンは、
インテリアデザイナー。
コマーシャルインテリアの
「モダン」アールデコ様式で
有名。ヴィジュアル
アイデンティティ
プログラムは、サリー・
アン・オハロンの名前を
カ強く・簡潔に扱い、
仕事に対する彼女の姿勢を
表現するようにした。
ロゴは事務用品、パンフレット
フォルダーなどに
使われている。

FOODTOWN SUPERMARKETS LIMITED

Foodtown's supermarket in Palmerston North is New Zealand's first 'lifestyle supermarket'.
It sells not only products but service, fun, convenience, excitement, fashion and colour.
It is an excellent example of image power at its most potent. As designers, we were
involved in every aspect of the development of the store, the first of many Foodtown
'lifestyle supermarkets'. It is warm, friendly, spacious and airy. The interiors are neutral
to allow the products to speak for themselves. Expanded aisles and gondola lighting
allow greater shopping comfort. The Foodtown symbol and all the interior signage has a
sense of being smooth, round and approachable. At the checkouts, a particular
design for the indicators was implemented to allow an uninterrupted view of each aisle

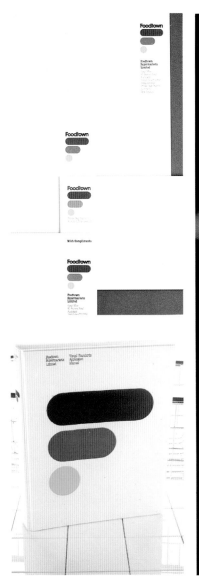

203

パーマストン・ノースにあるフードタウン・スーパーマーケットは、ニュージーランド最初のライフスタイルスーパーマーケット。つまり、商品だけでなく、サービス、娯楽、便利さ、ファッション、それに明るさを売り物にしているのだ。これはイメージが最大限の力を発揮したよい例である。店のデザインはあたたかく、親しみやすく、広々として、快適だ。インテリアそのものはニュートラルにして、商品自体が語り出すようにしてある。広い通路やゴンドララインティングも（商品棚の上に天井から吊り下げられた円筒形照明。円筒の中にサーチライトが入っている）快適なショッピングを約束する。フードタウンのシンボルマークと内部の標識は、流れるようにまろやかで、親しみやすい感じを持たせた。レジはそれぞれの入口が遠くからでもはっきりわかるよう特に注意してデザインするなど、工夫を凝らしている。デザイナーとしてわれわれは、最初から最後までかかわったこの店の開発に、ライフスタイルスーパーマーケットの先駆けとなったのである。

Soaps Toilet
Shaving needs
Toiletries
Towels
First Aid

GIANT STORES LIMITED

New Zealand's Giant Stores operate a large lifestyle hypermart which serves the community with non-food items and general merchandise in a self-serve environment. As it is part of the Foodtown group of supermarkets, it was important that the visual identity program projected an integrated look. The interiors of the store provide a bright, cheerful atmosphere and the symbol and graphics were used on bags, price tags, stationery items and signage.

ニュージーランドのジャイアント
ストアーズは食料品以外の、しゃれた
日常雑貨を売る大規模なセルフサービス式
ハイパーマートである。ジャイアント
ストアーズはフードタウン・スーパー
マーケット・グループの一員であり、
そのヴィジュアルアイデンティティプログラムに
「一員である」という含みを
持たせることが重要であった。
店内のインテリアは明るい陽気な
雰囲気を持っておりシンボルマークと
グラフィックは、バッグ、商札、
事務用品、サイニッジに
使われている。

FIRST CAPITAL CORPORATION

First Capital Corporation is a highly professional and well respected company offering financial and property investment services. The company's major clients are shareholders, employees and government bodies connected with the finance industry. The directors of First Capital Corporation have a methodical, systematic and disciplined approach to business and have firmly established a place in the international world of finance. The visual identity program we developed First Capital Corporation clearly reflects the company's philosophy and has been reproduced on a wide range of stationery items and signage

ファースト・キャピタル・コーポレイションは、金融および不動産投資に関する質の高いサービスで有名な企業。主な顧客は、株主、一般投資家、金融関係の政府機関。重役陣は、確立した方法論を持ち、組織的にかつ規律ある態度で仕事に臨んでいる。開発したヴィジュアルアイデンティティプログラムは、この哲学を明確に反映し、多くの事務用品や看板に適用されている。

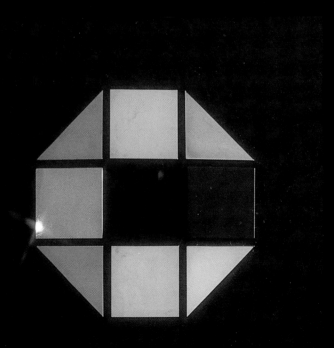

APPLIED RESEARCH CORPORATION

The Applied Research Corporation of Singapore is an organisation controlled by the National University of Singapore. As well as being a major research facility, ARC advises industry of appropriate areas of development to increase their competitiveness locally and overseas. The corporation's central philosophical function is to make inquiry, to question. By creating a question mark and including it in the logo design, this esoteric yet major aspect of ARC's identity is projected within an accessible image

シンガポールのアプライド・リサーチ・コーポレーションは国立大学の一部であり、大きな研究組織であるだけでなく、産業に対して、国内外での競争力を高めるための助言を行なう。その中心的な活動は問いかけ、探求することである。疑問符をデザインし、ロゴデザインに組み込むことにより、今まであまり目立たなかったアプライド・リサーチ・コーポレーションの存在が、親しみやすいかたちの中に投影されることになった。

A book this size requires an enormous amount of co ordination and organisation by a large number of people. Firstly, we would like to acknowledge the contribution made to the projects shown in these pages by all the people who have worked within Cato Design Inc over the past 17 years. We would also like to thank those people whose special skills we have employed from outside the company

Apart from these efforts, our clients deserve recognition for their understanding of our aims

We would like to acknowledge David Webster, Howard Russell and Riko Samejima for editorial assistance, Hiro Tokita for the Japanese translations, Jane Christmas for writing the book and John Banagan for the majority of the photographs.

208

これだけの本を出すためには、多くの人々の協力とまとまりが必要だった。まずケン・ケイトー・デザイン・カンパニーでこれまでの一七年間ずっと働いてきたスタッフ全員の努力がある。さらに社外から力を貸して下さった人々がいる。記して感謝したい。

これらの人々の努力の他、クライアントの方々もわれわれの目標を理解し協力して下さった。ここでお礼を申し上げる。

また編集の面で、デイヴィッド・ウェブスター、ハワード・ラッセル、鮫島理子に、日本語への翻訳で時田正博に、そして文章をつけてくれたジェーン・クリスマスに、それぞれ謝意を表したい。

ビジネス・デザイン
1987年11月5日　初版第1刷発行

編者─────ケン・ケイトー©
発行者────久世利郎
発行所────株式会社グラフィック社
　　　　　　〒102　東京都千代田区九段北1-9-12
　　　　　　☎03(263)4318　振替・東京3-114345

定価─────12,500円

ISBN4-7661-0422-6　C3070　¥12500E
落丁・乱丁本はお取替え致します。

本書の収録内容の無断転載、複写、引用等を禁じます。